Salzburg, Austria

And the Salzburg Area

A Starting-Point Guide

Barry Sanders – writing as:

B G Preston

Salzburg, Austria

Copyright © 2022 by B G Preston / Barry Sanders

All rights reserved. No part of this book may be reproduced or transmitted in any form or by any means without written permission from the author via his Facebook page. www.Facebook.com/BGPreston.author or email address cincy3@gmail.com

ISBN: **9798845855060**

1st edition – September 2022

Acknowledgements: The author greatly appreciates Sandra Sanders' contributions. She provided substantial editorial assistance to ensure the accuracy of this work.

Photography: Photos and maps in the Starting-Point Guides are a mixture of those by the author and other sources such as Shutterstock, Wikimedia, and Google maps. No photograph or map in this work should be used without checking with the author first.

~ ~ ~ ~ ~ ~

Salzburg's "Love Lock" Bridge
The Marko-Feingold-Steg Footbridge over the Sallzach River.
(Also known as the Markart-Steg bridge)

Contents

Preface: The "Starting-Point" Traveler 1

1: Salzburg Overview 8

2: Traveling to Salzburg 20

3: When to Visit 26

4: Where to Stay in Salzburg 32

5: City & Region Discount Passes 42

6: Salzburg Area Tours 46

7: Points of Interest in Salzburg 55

8: Beer/Bier Houses & Gardens 88

9: Salt Mines Near Salzburg 93

10: Exciting Day Trips 101

Index of Sights in this Guide 114

Starting-Point Guides 116

~ ~ ~ ~ ~ ~

Preface: The "Starting-Point" Traveler
Some General Travel Suggestions

Introduction & Area Covered:

This Starting-Point guide is intended for travelers who wish to really get to know a city and the surrounding area and not just make it one quick stop on a tour through Austria, Germany, and the region. Oriented around the concept of using Salzburg as a basecamp for several days, this handbook provides guidance on sights both in town and some of the nearby towns, mountain excursions, and the Salzburg Lakes Region.

View of Salzburg's Historic Center (Alstadt) from Fortress Hohensalzburg

A Starting-Point Guide

This is not a complete guide to the entire **state of Salzburg** [1] or central Austria and the neighboring region of Bavaria. Such a guide would go beyond the suggested scope of staying in one town and having enjoyable day trips from there. Any destination beyond ninety minutes each way is not included here.

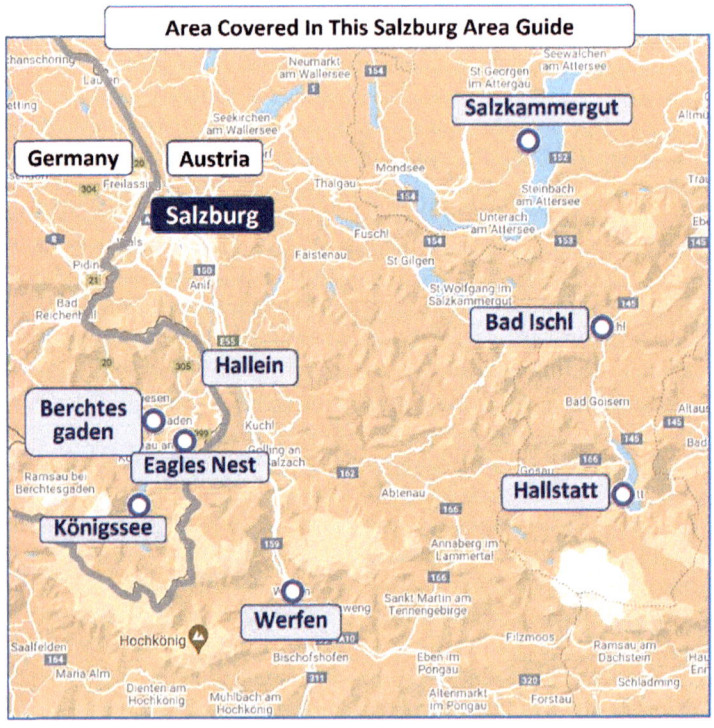

---

[1] **Salzburg State**: In addition to being the name of the city, Salzburg is also the name of this state in Austria. Not unlike North America's "New York City, New York."

The Ideal Itinerary:

The First Suggestion: If your travel schedule allows **plan on staying at least 2 nights in Salzburg.** Ideally, you will be able to stay as many as four nights. This is a delightful small city to stay in and is it easy to find your way out of town to the sights which beckon.

This is an area with a wonderful variety of destinations outside of town. Several days are needed to obtain even a moderate understanding of what the region has to offer.

A three-night itinerary would, for example, allow you to: (a) arrive mid-day on your first day and become oriented to the area around your lodging and explore some of the historic old town; (b) spend one full day in the city of Salzburg to discover several of the highlights; (c) spend one day in one of the more popular destinations such as Eagles Nest or one of the dramatic salt mines; then (d) head out to your next destination. If you were to add just one day to this stay, you could spend more time exploring the mountain areas and perhaps have a hiking or rafting adventure.

The Second Suggestion: If you are in town for four or more days, leave one day open and unplanned near the end of your stay. Build in a day in which you have not pre-booked any excursions or planned major activities. The reason for this is that, once there, you will discover places which you want to revisit or learn of new places which appeal to you. If you have a full schedule, you will lose this luxury.

Consider a City or Area Discount Card:

When staying in a city filled with attractions, it can be valuable to purchase a City Card, the Salzburg Card, or area card, the SalzburgerLand Card.

A Starting-Point Guide

Acquire one if you are likely to visit multiple attractions. Do not acquire one if you will only want to visit one or two attractions during your stay. These passes can always be purchased in the Tourist Office and are available online prior to your trip.

When visiting Salzburg, you will have options of purchasing the city card in increments of 24, 48, or 72 hours. Prices vary by the time of year you will be visiting. Salzburg also offers several packages which include a hotel stay. There are differences between the Salzburg Card and SalzburgerLand Card, but both are not needed due to substantial overlap. See chapter 5 for details between the two programs or check the websites at **www.Salzburg.info** and **www.SalzburgerLand.com.**

Visit the Tourist Office:

The tourist office website is: **www.Salzburg.info.** This is an excellent site which provides ability to book tours, buy a City Card, and download helpful maps.

Salzburg is a popular tourist destination, and the city does a great job of helping visitors including providing two offices in town:

Main Train Station: Look for the office near the station's main entrance hall. Given this location, personnel here are adept at not only promoting Salzburg, but also providing guidance on taking local and regional trains.

Preface – the Starting-Point Traveler

Mozartplatz: Near the entrance to Salzburg's "Old Town" is a small plaza, the "Mozartplatz." The office is located very close to the prominent statue of Mozart.

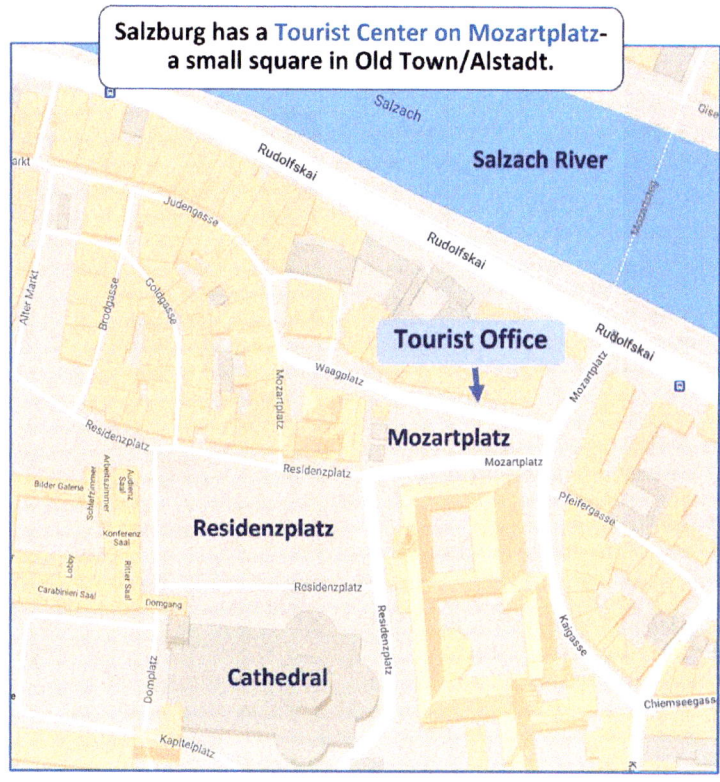

At the tourist office (or web site), you may find:
- Information on local transportation.
- Details on city passes.
- Helpful maps of the city and suggested walking tours.
- Obtain information on local and area tours and purchase tickets.

A Starting-Point Guide

Download some Apps: [2]

With the incredible array of apps for Apple and Android devices, almost every detail you will need to have for a great trip is available up to and including where to find public toilets. The apps range from those created by official agencies such as the Tourist Office and area train service to several which are put together by individual app developers. Following are a few recommended by the author.

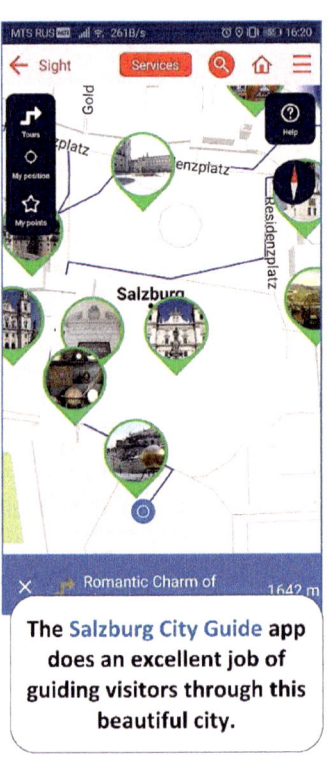

The **Salzburg City Guide** app does an excellent job of guiding visitors through this beautiful city.

- **Salzburg City Guide**: Provided by MyGuide.city. This app provides information on the area's attractions, transportation, restaurants, tours, shopping, and more. A very complete and well-rated app.

- **Salzburg Travel Guide**: Similar to the above Salzburg City Guide. This app is developed by etips and has maps, suggested walking routes, details on attractions and tours. (Note, there are several apps on Salzburg of this nature.)

---

[2] **No printed street maps in this guide.** This guidebook does not include street maps for the simple reason that the apps outlined here do a far superior job of providing map and interactive guidance than any printed guidebook or map can do.

Preface – the Starting-Point Traveler

- **Salzburg Mobil:** A helpful app for using the area's public transportation with routes and schedules.
- **ÖBB – Austria Trains:** If you are likely to travel around Austria on the area's trains, this app should be considered. It provides details on all routes and 40,000+ plus stations. Tickets and seat reservations may be made directly from this app.
- **Rome2Rio**: An excellent way to research all travel options including rental cars, trains, flying, bus, and taxi. The app provides the ability to purchase tickets directly online. A good option to this is the Trainline app.
- **Google Translate:** A must if you do not know any German. This app is a tremendous help when you need to communicate with non-English speaking locals.
- **Trip Advisor**: Probably the best overall app for finding details on most hotels, restaurants, excursions, and attractions.
- **Flush**: A very helpful app which provides guidance on where to find public toilets.

1: Salzburg Overview

Salzburg fits the image of a fairy-tale city in many ways and it is no wonder that it is such a popular destination. The destination in this case is far more than this attractive small city, it is the neighboring area as well. Visitors to Salzburg are treated to:

- Delightful Old Town with meandering lanes.
- Beer gardens & breweries.
- Imposing fortress and palace.
- Cultural landmarks including Mozart and the *Sound of Music*.
- Scenic parks ranging from formal to forest walks.
- Majestic mountain-top excursions.
- Intriguing salt & ice caves.
- River excursions.
- More trails and outdoor sports opportunities than you could count.

> **What are the "downsides" to visiting here?**
> - It can be crowded.
> - There is so much to see and do it can be a bit daunting.
> - This area is not cheap.

This is one city where some advance planning is highly suggested, especially if you are here for just a day or two. With so many choices of sights and activities, some understanding of which to select to fit your preferences will help ensure a successful visit.

Salzburg City & Region Overview

View of Old Town Salzburg - framed by nearby mountains.
Photo Source: Franganillo - Wikimedia

Salzburg is much more than the frequently promoted Mozart and *Sound of Music* history found here. Situated in a river valley in north-central Austria, it is framed by the foothills of the Alps and the border with Germany's Bavarian region. One of the pleasures of exploring this city is seeing mountains around you which are often snowcapped.

Not only is the city framed by mountains, it is also overlooked by the impressive Hohensalzburg Fortress, an 11th century masterpiece. From almost every part of central Salzburg, this intriguing complex beckons to you. Chapter 7 outlines details on this and other leading points of interest.

> Salzburg is a UNESCO World Heritage City and is described as "A city of outstanding value to humanity."

A Starting-Point Guide

A fun way to explore Salzburg is to take a carriage ride.

This is a small city and you rarely are overwhelmed by heavy traffic or busy thoroughfares. To be fair, it is an active city and it does have fast-moving expressways bordering parts of the city. The central area where visitors are likely to spend their time, this just is not the case. It is also an impressively clean city and area which improves the feeling of safety and wellbeing when exploring here.

The Hohensalzburg Fortress in "Old Town/Altstadt" overlooking the Mirabell Gardens in "New Town/Neustadt."
Photo Source: Rafa Esteve - Wikimedia

The architecture here is largely Baroque, a style which started in Italy in the 17th century and was used to depict wealth and power. Many of the more notable buildings, such as the Mirabell Palace, were crafted in this style. As a result, this city puts on a refined air and you find architectural delights throughout the center of the city.

In all likelihood, most of your explorations will be in the fairly small area which is essentially Salzburg's "Old Town" or

"Altstadt" and the across-the-river neighbor of "New Town or "Neustadt." As a caution, different sources show differing definitions for where Neustadt's boundaries are. For simplicity in this guide, the Salzach River will be used as the separator between old and new.

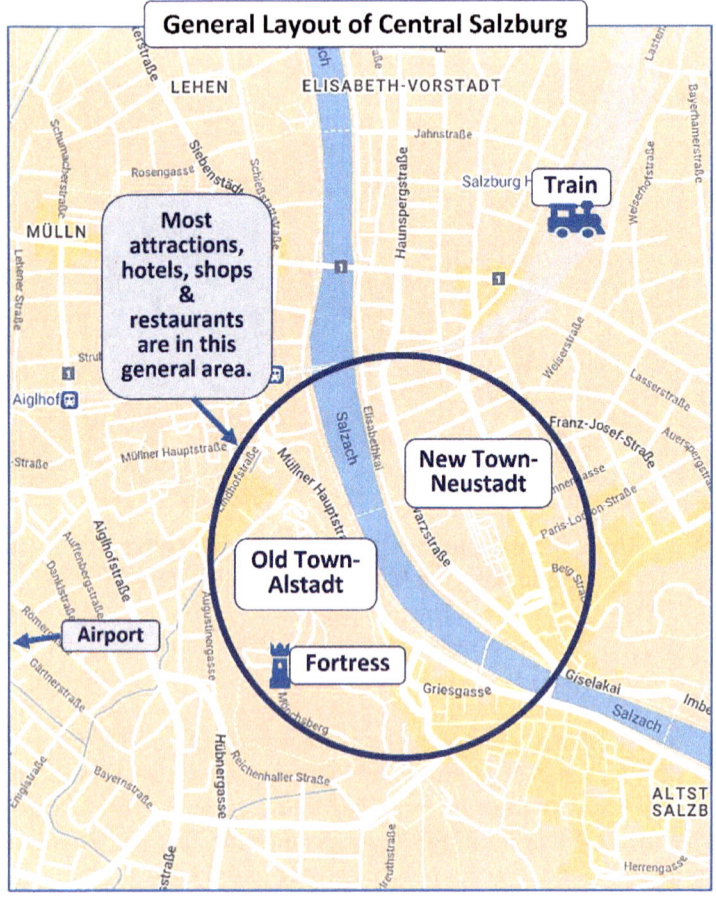

The Old Town is largely car free so if you, for example, take a taxi to here from the airport or train station, you are likely to be dropped off along the main boulevard along the river and not at a specific destination in the heart of Old Town/Altstadt.

Navigating around central Salzburg is easy to do on foot, although it is rare to find a straight path from one part of the historic center to another. This maze of narrow streets adds to the fun. With the river slicing through the center of town, and the fortress looking down on you, these landmarks help reduce the chance of your getting lost. But, if you did, you could find worst towns to get lost in and you won't have to go far to find your way once again.

The streets in "Old Town/Altstadt" are a joy to explore but can be crowded in the summer.
Photo Source: Diego Delso - Wikimedia

This is a city of historic treasures with no wrong way to start your explorations. The natural starting point for many will be the Hohensalzburg Fortress which overlooks Old Town. A visit there can include an enjoyable funicular ride up to the fortress. From there you can check out the beautiful city below and take

Fortress Hohensalzburg looms over Alstadt, Salzburg's historic center.
Photo Source: N. Karaneschev - Wikimedia Commons

Salzburg City & Region Overview

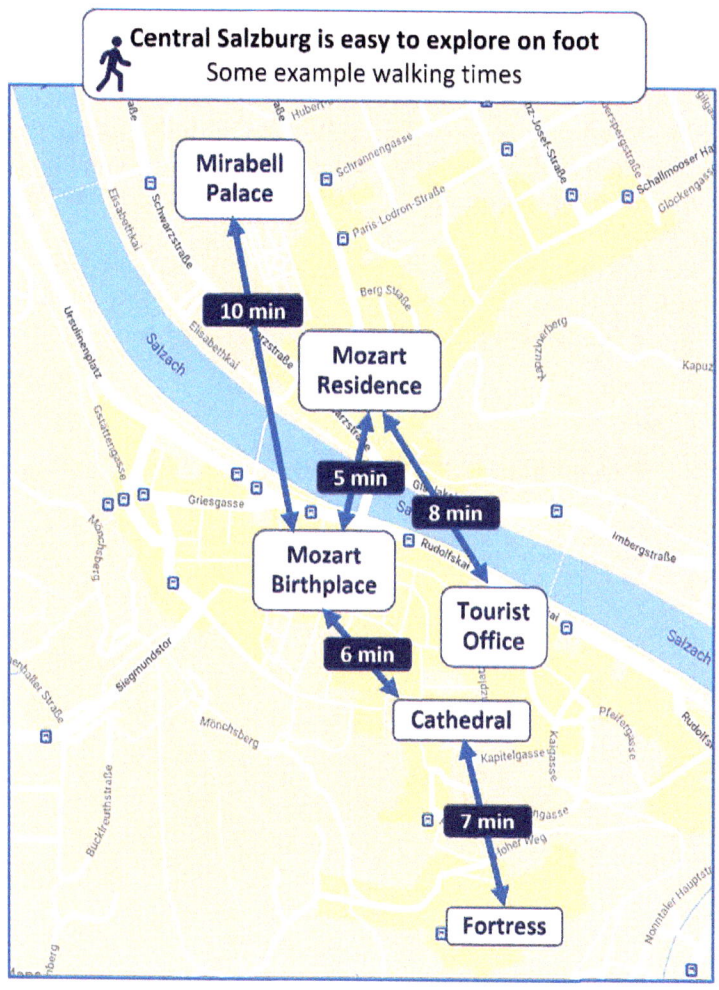

the opportunity to identify where some of your preferred destinations are located such as Mozart's birthplace, the Mirabell Palace, or the Cathedral.

Not all of the popular points-of-interest are right in Old Town or New Town. A few, such as Schloss Hellbrunn are slightly further afield. Chapter 7 outlines the details on these and other attractions in and near central Salzburg.

A quick note about language use here. If you are an English speaker and do not speak any German, you will generally be okay within central Salzburg. Still, having an understanding of some basic phrases or having a handy translator app available can be helpful.

Another plus when visiting here is that Austria uses the Euro which is helpful if you are visiting nearby Italy or Germany. Only Switzerland, which is close, uses a different currency.

City and Area General Information:

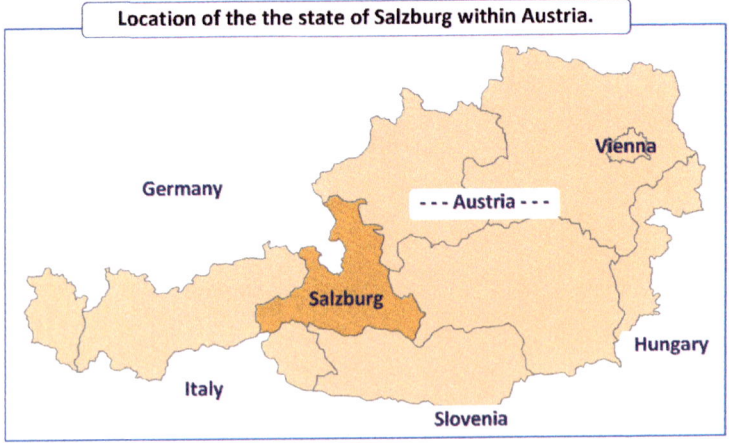

An understanding of the names used and geography of the city and area can be beneficial. Following are a few basic facts about this beautiful area which might prove useful.

- Salzburg Name: The name means "Salt Castle." An alternate spelling in German, "Salzburgschloss," is frequently found in literature. This name comes from the times when

Salzburg City & Region Overview

salt barges along the Salzach River were common and a central element of the area's economy.

- **Size:** It is Austria's fourth-largest city. The city population as of 2020 was 158,000. The three larger Austrian cities are: Vienna, Graz, and Linz. As a point of comparison, Vienna, Austria's largest city, has almost 2 million people, more than ten times Salzburg's population.

- **Capital of Salzburg:** Salzburg is the capital of the Austrian state of Salzburg. Austria has nine states and Salzburg is the 7th largest.

- **Elevation:** Salzburg's elevation is much less than its alpine setting would lead visitors to believe. It is only 1,390 feet (424 meters).

- **Nearby Mountains:** Salzburg sits along the northern edge of the Alps. Immediately to the south of the city (10 miles) is the alpine peak of Untersberg which stands 6,469 feet (1972 meters)

- **Student Population & Colleges**: Several colleges are based in Salzburg or have branches here. The largest is the University of Salzburg (often cited as the Paris Lodron University)

The University of Salzburg with Hohensalzburg Fortress overlooking it.
Photo Source: Diego Jorge Franganillo - Wikimedia

A Starting-Point Guide

with over 18,000 students. Given the large proportion of students here, Salzburg has a lively and youthful atmosphere.

- **WWII Damage**: When exploring this beautiful city, it is hard to visualize that nearly half of the buildings here were destroyed by Allied bombing in WWII. Luckily, many of the Baroque-style buildings survived.
- **Mozart:** The area's most famous citizens includes Wolfgang Mozart. He was born here in 1756 and his birth home is open for tours. He remained here until 1781 when he moved to Vienna. If you are in town when the Salzburg Festival is active, don't miss it as Mozart's music often takes center stage.

Highlights Near Salzburg:

One of the compelling reasons to stay here for several days is the incredible variety of natural and manmade sights which may be reached easily from Salzburg. Another bit of good news is many of these destinations are easy to reach by train, bus, or one of the many available tours.

Separate chapters are devoted to some of the biggest groupings of out-of-town attractions. There is a lot to choose from which is another reason for staying in this town for several days if your budget and schedule allow.

- Salt Mines & Mine Tours – chapter 9
- Day Trips to nearby Mountains and Towns - chapter 10

Salzburg City & Region Overview

There are many great day trip opportunities near Salzburg, such as Hallstatt town and lake shown here.

2: Traveling to Salzburg

Situated in the center of Austria, Salzburg is easy to reach from several neighboring cities and other countries. This chapter provides guidance for traveling to here by train or airplane.

If you are booking travel to and from here on your own, **use trains if possible.**

The scenery along the way is appealing and you can travel in a relaxed mode. Curiously, taking the train can often be faster than flying even though the actual transportation time can be longer. Trains take you directly from the center of one city to another, plus you have minimal check in and baggage collection time to deal with.

If you choose to fly, the Salzburg airport is only 15 minutes or less from the center of the city. Several transportation options into town are available.

Suggested Travel Planning App:

There are several excellent online sources to help plan your transportation. One of the better firms, which is highly recommended by the author, is "Rome2rio.com." This firm provides an excellent website and app to use when trying to plan local

Traveling to Salzburg

travel to Salzburg or any of the day-trip destinations cited here. It may also be used for almost every city in Europe.

Use this service to view travel options available such as train, flights, trams, bus, taxi, or self-drive. When choosing bus or train options, the ability to purchase tickets online is available. Schedules for trains and buses are provided with full details.

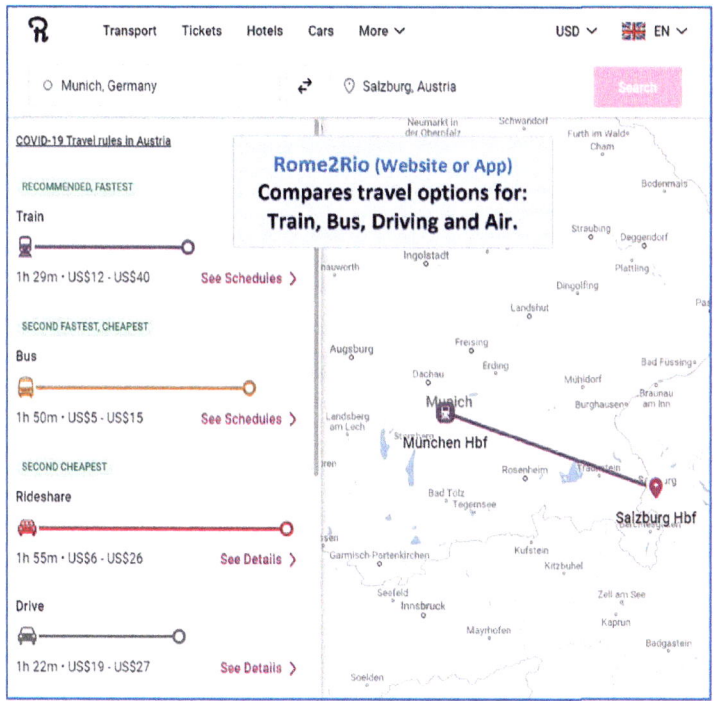

Arriving by Train:

Trains are often the best way to travel to Salzburg and many other cities and towns in the region. The map on the following page depicts typical travel times to here from major cities nearby.

A Starting-Point Guide

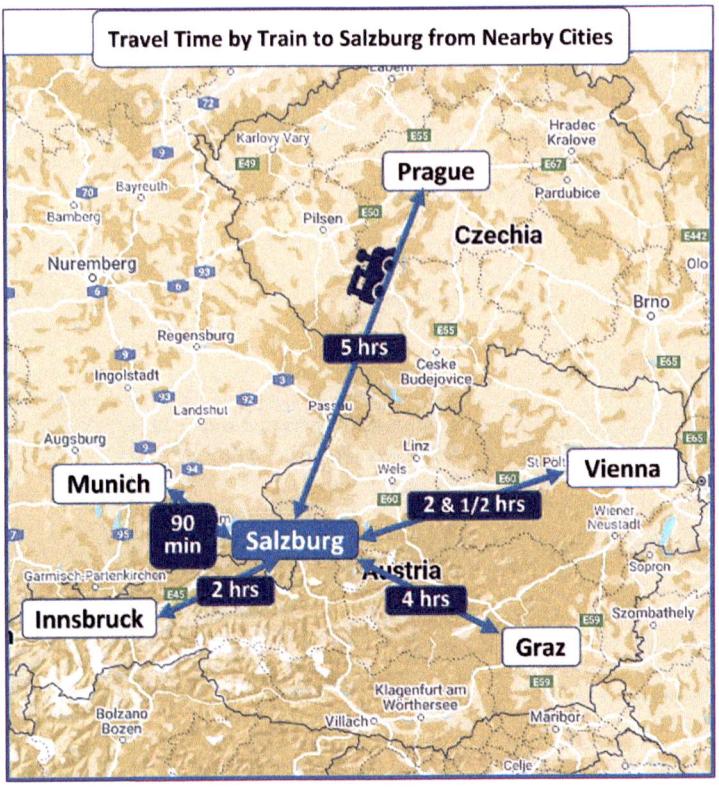

When coming into Salzburg by train you will arrive at the **Salzburg Hbf** (Hauptbahnhof) **station.** This station is a short distance north of central and Old Town Salzburg. See the map on page 24 which indicates where the station is in relationship to other areas of town. This station is a 15-minute or greater walk into central Strasbourg and is not advised as some of it is along busy roadways.

Once you arrive at the station, there are buses and taxis immediately outside. A branch of the Tourist Office is also here where the personnel can help you learn the system. If you have just arrived with luggage in hand, **consider taking a taxi** as it greatly adds to convenience and reduces stress. Later, once you have settled in, you can learn the local transportation network at your leisure.

The Salzburg Hauptbahnhof Train Station
A shopping center connects to this station and many bus lines stop right out front.
Photo Source: H. Ortner - Wikimedia Commons

Hop-On Bus from the Train Station.

If you come into Salzburg for just one day, consider catching the "Hop-On/Hop-Off" bus at the train station.

It can also be helpful to note that there is a shopping center connected to the train station, the Forum 1 Center. This can be very handy if you want to stock up on any items you forgot to pack or just pick up some snacks. This center's website is Forum1.at.

Booking train tickets. Given the popularity of travel to Salzburg from Munich and Vienna, advance purchase of train tickets should be

A Starting-Point Guide

considered, especially in high season or when the Salzburg Festival is happening. If you have not purchased tickets in advance, there are convenient ticket booths available at the train station.

Tickets may be purchased from several sources including: **TheTrainline.com, rome2Rio.com,** and others.

Arriving by Air:

The Salzburg airport (SZG) is located 10 to 15 minutes west of the city. Time varies based on your in destination in town and is quite close to the border with Germany. This is an easy trip into town and you will rarely encounter heavy traffic along the

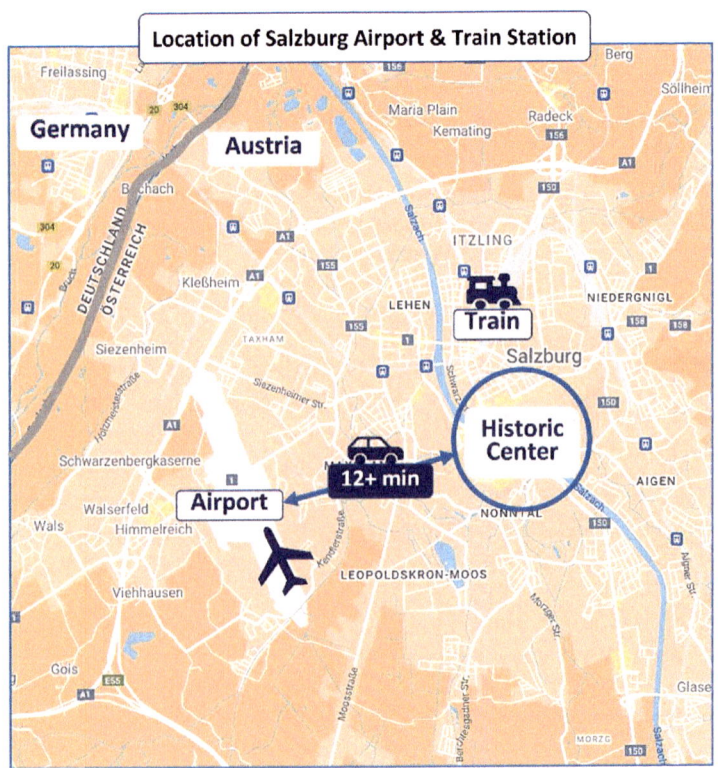

way. The airport is a modest size as there are only two-dozen or so flights per day, so it is rarely crowded. It is easy to navigate through. The website for the airport is **www.Salzburg-Airport.com.**

Ground Transportation from the Airport: As with most airports, you have several options for traveling into town from the airport. Also, given the modest size of the Salzburg airport, finding these services is easy. Available modes of transportation include bus, shuttle, taxis, and rental cars.

- **Bus:** This is the least expensive travel option. Two different lines head into town from the airport. They each run every 10 to 20 minutes, so there is rarely a long wait. Bus #2 heads directly to the main train station, which is handy if you will catch a train after flying into town. Bus #10 goes into the heart of Salzburg, but it makes several stops which can be confusing if you do not know the area. Bus tickets may be purchased from a machine near the bus stop, or the Newscorner shop in the airport sells tickets. If you have pre-purchased a Salzburg Card, travel is free.

- **Taxis & Shuttles**: Several different taxi services are available and there is rarely a need to book in advance. Some taxi services focus on travel into Salzburg, others will take you to nearby towns or resorts. Cost for a taxi into town will be roughly €15 to €20, but will vary based on your destination. This option provides the distinct advantages of it being the shortest time and you are taken directly to your lodging which greatly adds to the convenience. If you wish to book in advance, one of the many options is the local taxi company, Salzburg Taxi: **www.Taxi.at.**

~ ~ ~ ~ ~ ~

3: When to Visit

Like most areas in Europe, your best times to visit Salzburg are spring and fall, especially if you wish to avoid crowds. If you are not averse to the multitudes of tourists in the summer, or frosty air in the winter, there really is no bad time to visit this charming town and city. Each season certainly has its own positives and negatives, but do not hold back on visiting here simply because it may not be an optimum season.

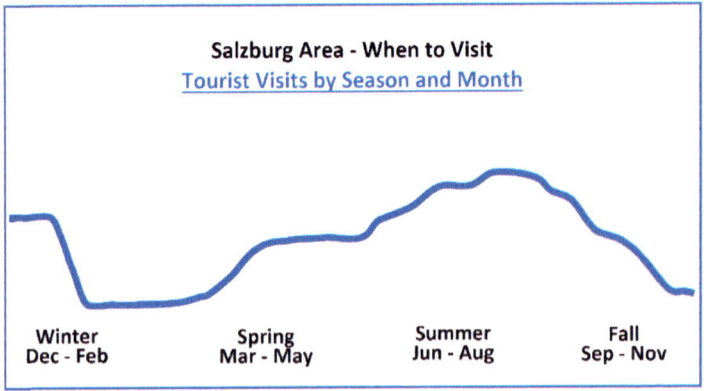

Officially, the climate here is defined as "Moderately Continental." Aside from the cold air which finds its way down from the Alps in the winter, one negative to be aware of is that cold wind gusts can funnel their way through this valley and town.

Rain and snow are common throughout the year. An average year will bring around 48 inches. Curiously, the months with the most frequent rain are late Spring through mid-August. During this period, some level of rain is likely to occur about every other day. (See climate chart on page 28)

Winter in Salzburg brings its own special beauty.
Photo Source: Gerhard Mauracher - Wikimedia

Some Seasonal Considerations:

Winter (Dec – Feb): This area can be very cold and gray from the start of the year to late February. Snow is common, but not so much as to inhibit travel. Many tours and tourist activities will be closed at this time of year. On the positive side, hotel rates are low and tourist crowds are non-existent during January and February. If you enjoy winter sports, there are several downhill and cross-country skiing opportunities in the area.

Spring (Mar-May): March will be much like February with cold and gray days and there is little tourism. A perfect time to venture out for winter activities as temps are better than in the dead of winter. By mid-April, tourism is starting to ramp up and tours which were not available in the winter start up again. Hotel rates, while not as low as winter, are generally good.

Summer (Jun-to-Aug): Summers in Salzburg and the region can be beautiful but crowded. Your chances of being able to explore the city or nearby areas with favorable weather are high. A perfect time to take a hike or explore the area's hillside and mountain retreats. On the downside, this is the most expensive time in the area for lodging. Every tour and tourist activity will be open which can greatly add to the fun you have when visiting.

Fall (Sep-Nov): Weather is generally pleasant with cool to warm temperatures. Rain chance is low in September and October. Most shops and tours will be open through October. Hotel rates decrease from their summer highs. All-in-all, probably the best time to visit here.

Typical Climate by Month:

Average Salzburg Climate by Month [3]			
Month		Avg High	Avg Low	Avg Precip
Jan	☹	38 F / 3 C	25 F / -4 C	2.3 inches
Feb	☹	42 F / 5 C	27 F / -3 C	2.1 inches
Mar	😐	50 F / 10 C	33 F / 1 C	3.4 inches
Apr	😐	59 F / 15 C	40 F / 4 C	3.1 inches

---

[3] **Climate Data Source:** Wikipedia.com

When to Visit

Average Salzburg Climate by Month [3]			
Month		Avg High	Avg Low	Avg Precip
May	☺	69 F / 20 C	48 F / 9 C	4.5 inches
Jun	☺	73 F / 23 C	54 F / 12 C	5.9 inches
Jul	☺	73 F / 23 C	57 F / 14 C	6.2 inches
Aug	☺	76 F / 24 C	57 F / 14 C	6.5 inches
Sep	☺	68 F / 20 C	51 F / 10 C	4.4 inches
Oct	😐	59 F / 15 C	43 F / 6 C	2.9 inches
Nov	😐	47 F / 8 C	34 F / 1 C	2.8 inches
Dec	☹	39 F / 4 C	28 F / -3 C	2.8 inches

Major Festivals and Events in Salzburg:

There are several popular events in and near Salzburg each year. Visiting one of these can be a great addition to a tour of the area especially as many of the events put the area's culture and cuisine on display. The only moderate downsides are the added crowds and increased lodging rates for major events. Information on some of the leading events which have broad appeal follow.

The websites **www.Salzburg.info** and **www.Visit-Salzburg.net** provide lists of events, concerts, and festivals around the city and area. Details on location and timing are provided along with the ability to purchase tickets. In many cases, if you hold a Salzburg Card (see chapter 5), you will be eligible for a discount.

Winter:

- **Salzburg Advent Festival / Salzburger Christkinklmarkt:** This is one of the most popular Christmas and Advent markets in Europe. The setting is in several attractive and historic plazas in town. With a likely coating of snow, it is the perfect place to get in the holiday spirit. There are several events and markets, such as the one on Mirabellplatz and the main "Christkindlmarkt," held in Old Town. Dates typ-

The Salzburg Advent Festival & Christmas Market is a delight.

ically are late November to January 1. Be sure to book lodging in advance as this is a popular set of events and hotels book up quickly. The website for this popular event is www.ChristKindlMarkt.co.at.

- **Mozart Week:** Mozart was born on January 28 and the city celebrates this event for a bit over a week each year in late January to early February. Several concerts are held at this time to honor his legacy.[4]

Spring/Summer:

- **The Salzburg Festival/Salzburger Festspiele:** This is Salzburg's most prominent festival. Held over several weeks from late July through August. This is a festival celebrating stage and music and you will find a wide array of concerts and plays. Venues range from the city's major theaters to street performers. Be sure to book tickets in advance. Full details may be found at: www.SalzburgerFestspiele.at.

-
- **Aspects Salzburg/Aspekte Festival**: Held in mid-March. The focus on this music event is on contemporary music. Each year there are numerous concerts held in a variety of venues. Full details may be found at: www.Aspetke-Salzburg.com.

---

[4] **Mozart Dinner Concerts:** If you are not in Salzburg when his Birthday is celebrated, don't worry as you may still attend an enjoyable concert of his music. Mozart Dinner Concerts are a popular event which occur most of the year. These are fun and highly recommended. Tickets may be booked via the Salzburg.Info website.

4: Where to Stay in Salzburg

Where you choose to stay when visiting a new city is essentially a personal choice. You may prefer hotels or rental apartments, or picking a place guided by your budget may be critical to you.

Regardless of the motives which drive your selection or the type of accommodation you prefer, the "Where in town should I stay?" question is critical to helping you have an enjoyable visit.

Budget and accommodation-type issues aside, the following criteria may be of importance to you:

- Convenience to historical sites, restaurants, shopping.
- Convenience to transportation.
- Noise levels around where you will stay.

Author's Recommendation:
If your budget allows, stay in the center of the historic area in either Old Town or New Town.

This guide does not provide details on all the hotels in Salzburg as there are too many to describe. There are many fine and dynamic online sources such as Trip Advisor, Booking.com, and others which provide far more detail than can be provided here. These sites will provide answers to every question you may have about a property and allow you to make reservations once you have made your selection.

Quality lodging of all types can be found throughout the Salzburg area. To help you in your selection, this guide outlines

Where to Stay in Salzburg

two subsets of central Salzburg to consider with a focus on hotels instead of rental apartments. Many other sectors of town have fine lodging such as near the train station or closer to the airport. These are not addressed here as the properties do not meet the basic criteria of convenience to the heart of town.

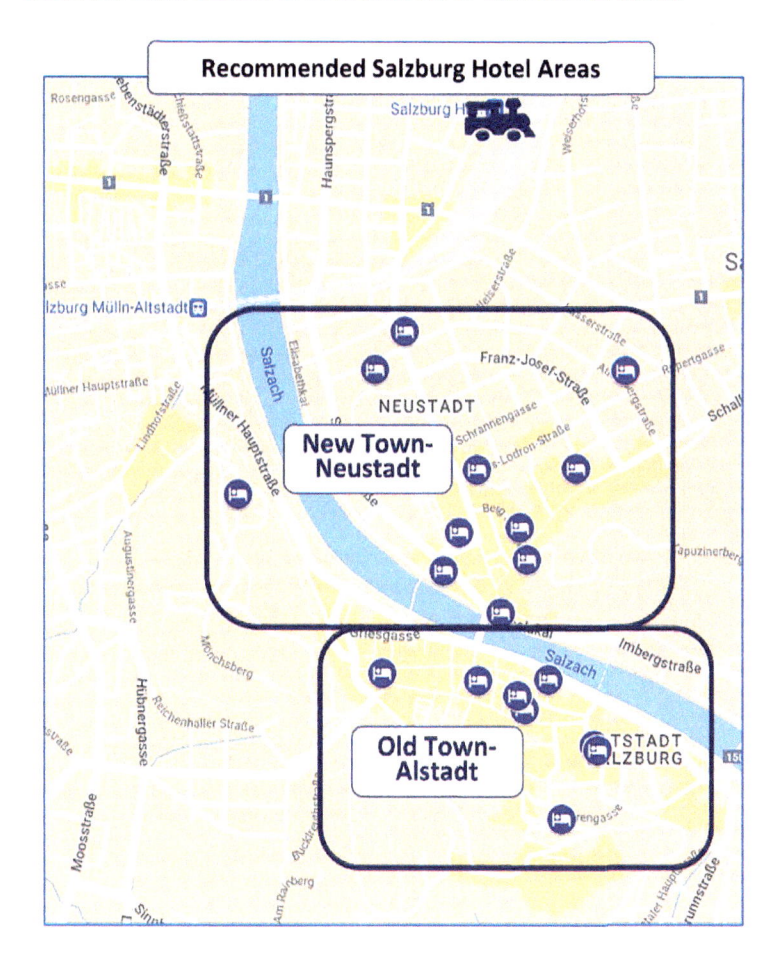

Recommended Salzburg Hotel Areas

New Town-Neustadt

Old Town-Alstadt

While two areas are detailed here, they are quite similar in they are very close to attractions, restaurants, and shopping. The

New Town/Neustadt area does offer advantages of better access to parking and it is closer to the train station. With the easier access to New Town for cars, this section also has the disadvantage of increased traffic and road noise. Bottom-line, if you are not worrying about ease of access to a vehicle, either area of town provides a great experience.

If you have a healthy budget, consider the Hotel Sacher. Located on the river with views of old town and the fortress.
Photo Source: M Paraskevas - Wikimedia

New Town Area / Neustadt:[5]

Neustadt is the section of town south of the train station by a half-mile or so and on Salzach River's right bank. This area is known for the Mirabell Palace & Gardens/Schloss Mirabell, a large farmers market, and Mozart's home. If you enjoy short

---

[5] **Staying at Villa Trapp:** This previous residence of the Trapp family from the *Sound of Music* was an active hotel. Recently it has shut down and, as of this writing, is no longer available to book lodging.

hikes, there is easy access to the hills and trails immediately to the south. Several lookouts provide great views of the city and neighboring mountains. There are many restaurants here and several beer gardens. [6]

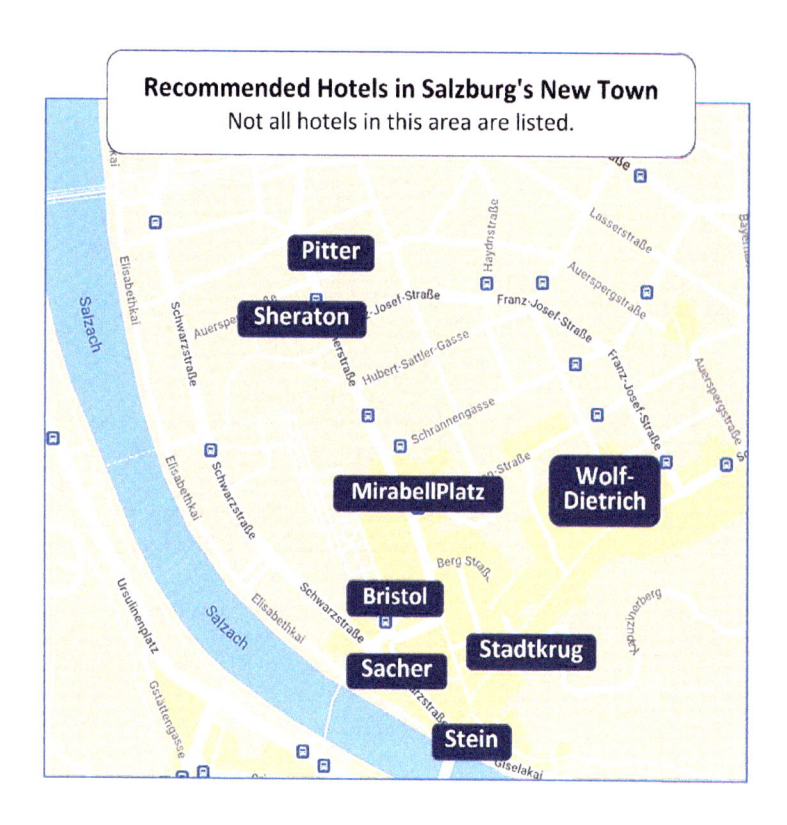

Recommended Hotels in Salzburg's New Town
Not all hotels in this area are listed.

- Pitter
- Sheraton
- MirabellPlatz
- Wolf-Dietrich
- Bristol
- Stadtkrug
- Sacher
- Stein

---

[6] **Hotel Ratings:** All hotel ratings in this guide are a composite of ratings from personal experiences, travel blogs and several popular sites such as Trip Advisor, Booking.com, Hotels.com, and others.

Suggested Lodging in New Town

(All selected lodging has 3.5 or better rating)

Hotel	Address & Details	Rating
Alstadt Hotel Stadtkrug	Linzer G 20 Boutique hotel with restaurant tucked away on a pleasant pedestrian shopping lane with many shops and restaurants nearby. **www.Stadtkrug.at**	4 stars
Hotel am Mirabellplatz	Paris-Lodron-Straße 1 Very central, near Mirabell Gardens. A bit upscale with multiple dining options. This is an historic property with an elegant feel. **www.ImLauer.com**	4 stars
Hotel Bristol Salzburg	Makartplatz 4 Upscale in every way. Elegant property with large rooms and suites and highly praised level of service. **www.Bristol-Salzburg.at**	5 stars
Hotel Sacher Salzburg	Schwarzstraße 5-7 Great location on the Salzach River with views across to old town and the fortress. A 5-star property in all regards. **www.Sacher.com**	5 stars
Hotel Stein	Giselaki 3 Another quality hotel and restaurant along the river with excellent views of Old Town and the Fortress. **www.HotelStein.at**	4 stars

Suggested Lodging in New Town

(All selected lodging has 3.5 or better rating)

Hotel	Address & Details	Rating
Hotel Wolf-Dietrich	Wolf-Dietrich-Straße 7 Situated in a pedestrian shopping zone, this mid-size property is convenient to shops, restaurants, and hikes up the hill which overlooks the town. **www.Salzburg-Hotel.at**	4 stars
Imlauer Hotel Pitter	Rainerstraße 6 Close to the convention center which is helpful if you are attending a conference. The sky bar is a great feature with views of the fortress and city. **www.Imlauer.com**	4 stars
Sheraton Grand Salzburg	Auerspergstraße 4 A large, full-service hotel near Schloss Mirabell and gardens, but in a business district and not the tourist center. Parking available. **www.Marriott.com**	4.5 stars

~ ~ ~ ~ ~ ~

A Starting-Point Guide

Old Town / Alstadt Area:

An ideal area to stay if you like to be right in the heart of history and the city's most prominent attractions. Most properties here are small to moderate in size and most excel in character. This is not a cheap area to stay. Imagine being in the shadow of a fortress on a hill overlooking your inn and near some of Austria's best beer gardens and more restaurants than you can count.

Recommended Hotels in Salzburg's Old Town / Altstadt
Not all hotels in this area are listed.

- Goldener Hirsch
- Hotel Elefant
- Radisson Blu
- Hotel Goldgasse
- Haus St. Benedikt
- Altstadt Hotel
- Weisses Kreuz

Stay in an active monastery, Haus St. Benedikt, for a unique lodging experience.
Photo Source: Edelsider · Wikimedia

Suggested Lodging in Salzburg's Old Town[7]		
(All suggested lodging is rated at 3.5 stars or greater)		
Restaurant	Address & Details	Rating
Alstadthotel Weisse Taube	Kaigasse 9	4 stars
	A modest-sized property with 31 rooms. Right in the center of Old Town and near Mozartplatz.	
	www.WeisseTaube.at	

---

[7] **Hotels Listed:** This is a popular area with numerous hotels, inns, and private rentals of all sizes and quality ratings. The properties listed here are intended to provide a cross-section of the well-rated lodging types and experiences available here. Other properties may be just as high in quality, but have not risen to the top of the rankings for this section of town.

Suggested Lodging in Salzburg's Old Town[7]

(All suggested lodging is rated at 3.5 stars or greater)

Restaurant	Address & Details	Rating
Haus St. Benedikt	Toscaninhof 1 An active monastery, with rooms and dining in one part of the large building. A unique and affordable experience. A bit spartan, but the location at the foot of the fortress can't be beat.	4 stars
Hotel Elefant	Sigmund-Haffner-Gasse 4 Tucked away on a narrow lane in old town, this pleasant property would be easy to miss. A boutique inn with character and the name "Elephant" is reflected in the décor. www.HotelElefant.at	4 stars
Hotel Goldener Hirsch	Goldgasse 10 The movie and theater décor creates a fun atmosphere in this small luxury property. www.HotelGoldGasse.at	4.5 stars
Radisson Blu Hotel Alstadt	Rudolfskai 28 A large property for old town. Tons of character and views of the river. 5-star in every regard. www.RadissonHotels.com	5 stars
Townhouse Weisses Kreuz	Bierjodlgasse 6 Small, intimate property with character and a great patio. Near the University. www.Townhouse-Weisses-Kreuz.at	3.5 stars

Staying near the Train Station:

Often, selecting a property near the main train station is a good idea if you are likely to take day trips by train or have an early departure.

In the case of Salzburg, <u>this is not recommended</u> as the area near the train station has little to offer visitors aside from the large Forum 1 shopping center adjacent to the station. It is primarily a business and apartment-block district.

5: City & Region Discount Passes

If you will be staying in Salzburg or the area and devoting multiple days to activities and tours here, you should consider purchasing one of the available discount passes.

These passes provide value and convenience **IF** you plan on visiting multiple museums or similar attractions. They are fairly expensive, so do not purchase one if you will be spending your time simply exploring the town, shopping, or enjoying outdoor activities.

Two Discount Travel Cards to Consider

In Salzburg, there are two prominent discount programs, the **Salzburg Card** and the **Salzburger Land Card**. At first look, these programs appear to be similar which can generate some confusion. While there is some overlap between the cards, the basic differences are the areas covered and duration. The Salzburg Card is for shorter durations of 1 to 3 days and the geographical focus is on Salzburg. The Salzburger Land Card is for a longer timeframe with a minimum of 6 days and includes attractions throughout the region, not just Salzburg. Some details follow.

Salzburg & Area Passes

Tours of Hellbrunn Palace are included in each of the passes

The Salzburg Card:
- Available for periods of 24, 48, or 72 hours.
- Area of focus is Salzburg with some nearby adventures.
- Coverage includes most Salzburg museums and city attractions. There is a mix of free and discounted admissions.
- Discounts on many tours to nearby attractions such as Salt Mine tours or Sound of Music tours.
- City transportation is included.
- Discounts to area entertainment such as Mozart concerts and beer garden tours.
- Options of packages including hotel stays in Salzburg are available.

SalzburgerLand Card:
- Days covered include choice of 6 or 12 days.
- Geographical coverage is for the region with Salzburg being only one of many cities included in the pass.

A Starting-Point Guide

- Most area museums are included with either free or discounted admissions.
- Many outdoor adventures are included. This is valid for longer periods of time than the Salzburg Card with options of 6 days and 12 days. Geographical coverage includes Salzburg and much of the surrounding area.
- Discounts to many different tours in the region are provided with this card.

Cost & Where to Purchase:

Discount Card Price Comparison[8]		
(Adult rates compared. Both programs also have discounted children's rates. Child rates are roughly ½ of the adult rate.)		
Period of Time	**Salzburg Card[9]**	**SalzburgerLand Card**
24 Hours	€30	n/a
48 Hours	€39	
72 Hours	€45	
6 Days	n/a	€82
12 Days		€98

---

[8] **Card Pricing** Note: All prices cited here are as of Summer, 2022 and are subject to change. Rates for the Salzburg Card are for the high season of Spring, Summer, and Fall. Slightly lower rates are available in Winter.

[9] **Hotel Combo Packages**: Programs including hotel stays are not cited in this rate comparison. Check **www.Salzburg.Info** for details.

- **Salzburg Card:** Purchase from the Tourist Offices in Salzburg or from their website at www.Salzburg.Info. They may also be purchased from various online resellers.
- **SalzburgerLand Card:** Purchase from the website at Salzburgerland.com in advance of your trip. There is also a kiosk at the airport. Several hotels in the area have this card available. It is not available through the Salzburg Tourist Center.

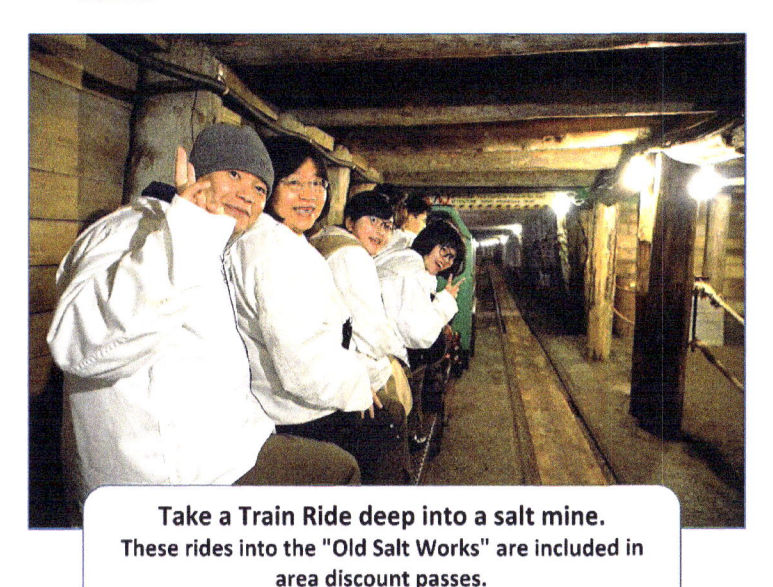

Take a Train Ride deep into a salt mine.
These rides into the "Old Salt Works" are included in area discount passes.
Photo Source: R. Swi-hymn - Wikimedia Commons

Discount Passes & Area Tours: Many tours are included in these passes. Some are free, if you purchase a pass, but in most cases, you simply receive a discount. The next chapter outlines some of the leading Salzburg area tour providers and several suggested tours to consider.

~ ~ ~ ~ ~ ~

6: Salzburg Area Tours[10]

Many companies provide tours of the city and the surrounding area. These tours include options such as city walking tours, food tastings, bike tours, and much more. In just looking at the listings of some of the popular tour reseller sites, there are over 500 different tours available out of Salzburg. Put another way, there is something here for everyone.

Strive to build in a tour of Salzburg or the neighboring towns or mountain

Guided Tours

The Salzburg.Info website is a good resource for city & area tours.

---

[10] **Tours for the independent-minded traveler & a personal note.** Like many individuals, the author has been disinclined to join in group tours, preferring to go it alone. This isn't always the best choice. After participating in some group tours with his family, he soon discovered how much could be gained from taking half-day and full-day area tours. Now, with each new city, the author builds in at least one day trip and, in every case, has found the experiences rewarding and educational.

destinations. These firms do all of the preparation and often are able to take you into locales which otherwise would have been missed.

Salzburg Tour Providers:

In addition to the Tourist Office, there are many agencies who provide tours here. In most cases, you can reserve and purchase a tour in advance from their website. This has a positive and negative element. On the positive side, you have the comfort of knowing you have locked in your tour and this component of your trip is set. On the negative side, if your plans change and you need to cancel, you may have difficulty in getting your money back.

There is substantial overlap in tours sold through these agencies and prices tend to be the same or similar.

Salzburg Tourist Office: www.Salzburg.Info. This is probably the best place to shop for tours as they offer a wide range of tours both into and near Salzburg. There is also the plus of being able to go directly to one of the Tourist Office locations in Salzburg to purchase tickets or work with them if plans change.

Most of these tours are from other providers and the Tourist Office resells them. This gives this office the ability to focus on tours from local providers and shift services as needs arise.

Grayline: www.Grayline.com (then select Salzburg). This firm is known world-wide for providing bus tours. Most of the tours they provide are their own and are not resold.

In Salzburg, one of their popular offerings is the Hop-On/Hop-Off buses. The primary Yellow Line guides visitors around central Salzburg. It is a good option for individuals coming into Salzburg for a one-day adventure by train as it stops at the train station. There is, on occasion, a Green Line route, but it is not always available. This route takes visitors to nearby mountain and lake areas.

Salzburg Hop-On Bus Tours

Bob's Special Tours: www.BobsTours.com – The name may seem out of place for Austria, but this is a well-rated tour firm which focuses on the Salzburg area. Their tours are also available from the Salzburg Tourist Office.

Bob's Tours provides good coverage of Salzburg, and area tours including some of Bavaria. Most tours are small groups and not large bus trips. They also offer private tours which can be customized to your preferences. This is a good source for some unique outdoor adventures such as area kayak tours.

Tours and Tour Companies

For a bit of fun, consider an amphibious cruise on the Salzach River.
Photo Source: SalzburgHighlights.com

Salzburg Highlights: **www.SalzburgHighlights.at** This is an excellent resource for some unusual and fun adventures ranging from dinner concerts to boat cruises. Salzburg Highlights has several river excursions including diner cruises.

If you are planning a big event or wedding here, this firm is noted for helping set up area weddings with local music and cuisine.

Salzburg Panorama Tours: **www.PanoramaTours.com** A local firm offering a good mix of "the usual" tours and several unique experiences. Several tours focus on the *Sound of Music,* other music and cuisine tours, and cooking classes.

In addition to bus tours with large groups, they also offer private tours where you can work with them to craft a tour to fit your preferences.

Viator: **www.Viator.com** or **www.TripAdvisor.com.** Viator is a subset of the popular Trip Advisor program. They do not offer their own tours but, rather resell a host of available tours. There are many to choose from. A strength of this firm is excellent customer service. [11]

Salzburg Tours to Consider:

Following are examples of Salzburg tours to consider. This list is far from comprehensive, but does provide a cross-section of the types of tours provided. Pricing for these tours is not included as it can frequently change. These tours fall into the broad groupings of:

1. Tours of Central Salzburg – walking, bus, and bicycle tours.
2. Food and Music – enjoy the area's cuisine and music with local experts.
3. *Sound of Music* Tours.
4. Outside of Salzburg – tours to area mountains, salt caves, and the lake area.

1 – Tours in Central Salzburg:

Walking Tours: Historical walking tour showing local architecture, Mozart's home, Mirabell Gardens, and more. A good orientation to major sights by a local expert. Time involved is around 2 hours. Low cost, group tours. Viator and Salzburg Panorama tours are some of the providers of this tour.

---

[11] **Other tour resellers like Viator**: Many other firms also resell these tours like this such as GetYourGuide.com, Booking.com, and others. If you have a preferred source for reserving hotels and tours, then in all probability, you can use them for many available tours in and around Salzburg.

Salzburg Cathedral Guided Tour: A 40-minute tour where you learn about this beautiful structure and its history. Tours include a visit to the historic crypt. Get Your Guide and Viator are two providers of this tour.

Hohensalzburg Fortress Tour. There is much to see and discover in this massive structure which overlooks the city including Royal apartments and arsenal. This is a lengthy, in-dept tour which includes the funicular ride and portions of old town. Duration will be around 3 hours. Check with the Tourist Office for details.

> Not all tours require a tour company.
> **Consider a Self-Guided Walking Tour**
> The Salzburg Tourist Office and website will provide maps for several suggested walking tours in central Salzburg. This is a great way to discover the city and do so on your own schedule.

Mozart's Life Walking Tour: Visit Mozart's birthplace, childhood home, Mirabell Gardens, and other locales which had an impact on this noted composer. The tour takes a bit over 2 hours and is offered by the Tourist Office and other providers.

2 – Food and Music Tours and Events:

Austrian Apple Strudel Cooking Class: For fun, especially with children or a group of friends, take a class in cooking this popular Austrian dish. Duration is just 90 minutes. This tour is offered through Viator.

Mozart Dinner Concert: Several music events and tours focusing on Mozart are available here. One of the popular events is a dinner at a hall in central Salzburg which includes a small group of musicians playing Mozart's favorites. Check the Tourist Office website or Viator for details.

Palace Concert: Held in the historic Marble Hall in the Mirabell Palace, this is a great way to listen to an evening of classical music in a near-perfect setting. This is a 90-minute concert which takes place in the evenings and does not include a meal. Check Viator for availability or book directly through **www.SalzburgPalace-Concerts.com.**

Beer Gardens & Brewery Tours: This is Austria and beer is a natural part of the fun. There are several beer gardens and breweries here. To help you find your way through them, several tours are offered. Check the **Salzburg.Info** website for details on the tours available. Also, for added guidance, check chapter 8 which outlines popular beer gardens in Salzburg.

3 – The *Sound of Music* Tours:

Nearly sixty years ago, the *Sound of Music* was filmed in and around Salzburg. The interest in this movie is still very strong and the city's tour companies provide many opportunities to have some fun with this.

Some *Sound of Music* Tours are limited to central Salzburg. Other tours also include bus or van travel out to filming locations in Austria's beautiful lake and mountain areas.

A *Sound of Music* Tour Bus
Photo Source: Wikimedia Commons

Sound of Music **Filming Locations:** [12]Tour of iconic filming locations both within Salzburg and out to the mountains where several scenes were filmed. A great way to meld some movie memories with tours of historic buildings in Salzburg and visits to the beautiful countryside. This is a half day tour which takes four hours.

Several variations of these tours are available. Some also include tours of area salt mines and these tours can last a full day. View the following to see which tour is best for you: Viator.com / Bobs Tours / Salzburg Panorama Tours.

4 – Tours outside of Salzburg:

Tours to attractions outside of Salzburg are where the many tour agencies provide the greatest value. Unless you have rented a car, many of the destinations are difficult to get to with public transportation. These tours take you directly to them. Often, they will combine a good mix of destinations to give you a varied set of experiences.

A small group, van tour such as those provided by Bob's Special Tours is a good way to visit the beautiful Austrian countryside.
Photo Source: Bob's Special Tours

---

[12] **Von Trapp Fun Fact:** If you are able to travel in the U.S. to Stowe in northern Vermont, you can visit the beautiful lodge and restaurant which the Trapp family set up after escaping Europe in the 1940s.

Many of these destinations are detailed in chapters 9 and 10 in this guide.

Listed below are four of the most popular destinations these tour companies include. Most agencies provide, or resell, the exact or similar offerings at similar prices. So, pick your preferred choice of provider such as Salzburg Panorama Tours, Viator, or Bobs Special Tours and have a great time.

Eagles Nest Tours: Visit Hitler's mountain retreat in the Bavarian Alps. Many tour options available, but count on a minimum of a 4-hour adventure. Full-day tours often include salt mine excursions. See chapter 10 for more info on the Eagles Nest.

Hallstatt, Austria and Lake District. Hallstatt, Austria is a beautiful town in Austria's lake district southeast from Salzburg. These tours often include a cable car trip into the mountains. Half-day and full-day tour options are available. See chapter 10 for details on Hallstatt.

Bavarian Mountains and Salt Mines: The region south of Salzburg is noted for its beautiful mountains. There are also many charming towns and intriguing salt mines to explore. These tours combine some of the best elements of these sights. Most tours are full day. See chapter 9 for details on the area's salt mines.

Großglockner Mountain: Travel south from Salzburg to Austria's highest mountain. This full-day tour focuses on the natural beauty of the area. Short walks are included.

~ ~ ~ ~ ~ ~

7: Points of Interest in Salzburg

When first coming to Salzburg, it is easy to assume the visit can easily be limited to simply exploring the Old Town and the fortress. It turns out that there is much more to see and do here.

The variety of attractions in and near the city center is quite diverse with something here for every interest. Within the historical center combination of New Town (Neustadt) and Old Town (Alstadt), there are over twenty points of interest. These range from attractive plazas which take only moments to appreciate to the hillside Fortress Honensalzburg which could easily take a full day to appreciate all it has to offer.

Several leading attractions, such as the Hellbrunn Palace (a noted *Sound of Music* filming location), are a bit outside of the historical center. Public transportation, the Hop on Bus, or an area tour will be needed to get to them.

> **Salzburg's "Hop On / Hop-Off" Bus**
>
> This service takes visitors to, or within easy walking distance of, all attractions outlined here.

This chapter outlines all of Salzburg's leading attractions with guidance on where each is located. Some destinations, such

A Starting-Point Guide

as the area's delightful beer gardens, are outlined in following chapters.

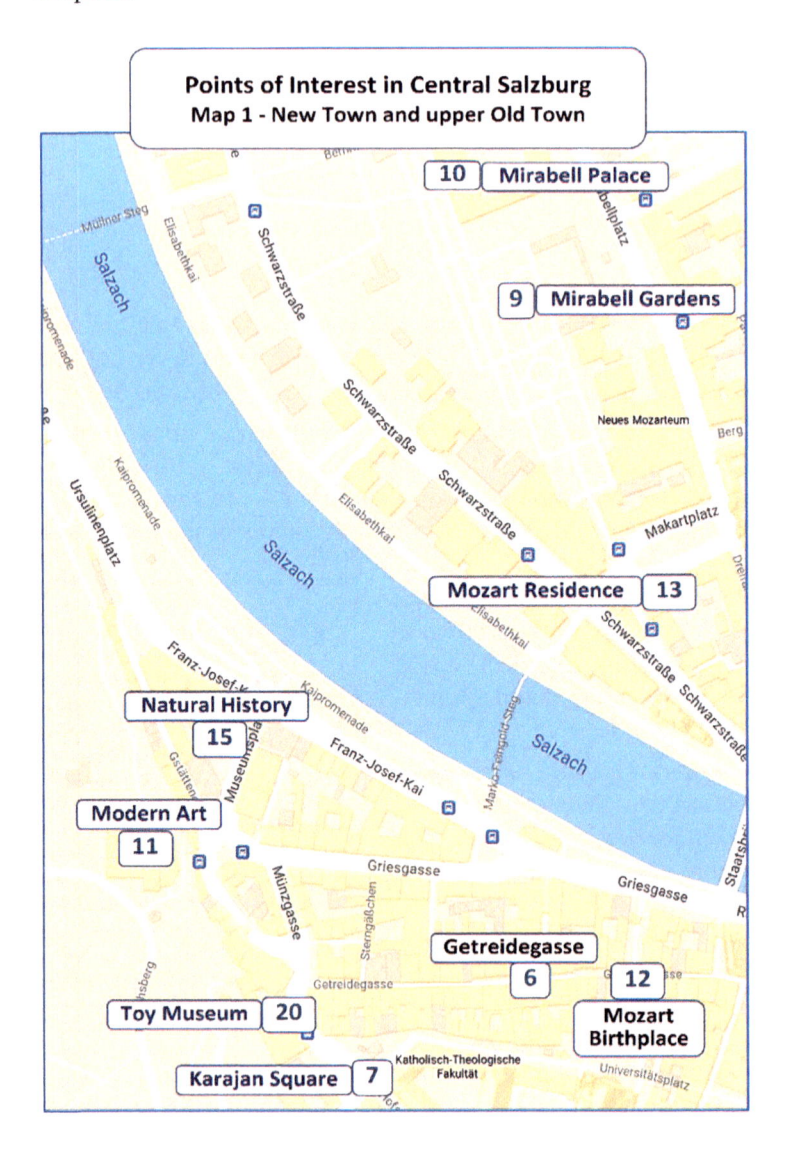

Points of Interest in Central Salzburg
Map 1 - New Town and upper Old Town

- 10 Mirabell Palace
- 9 Mirabell Gardens
- Mozart Residence 13
- Natural History 15
- Modern Art 11
- Getreidegasse 6
- 12 Mozart Birthplace
- Toy Museum 20
- Karajan Square 7

Points of Interest in Salzburg

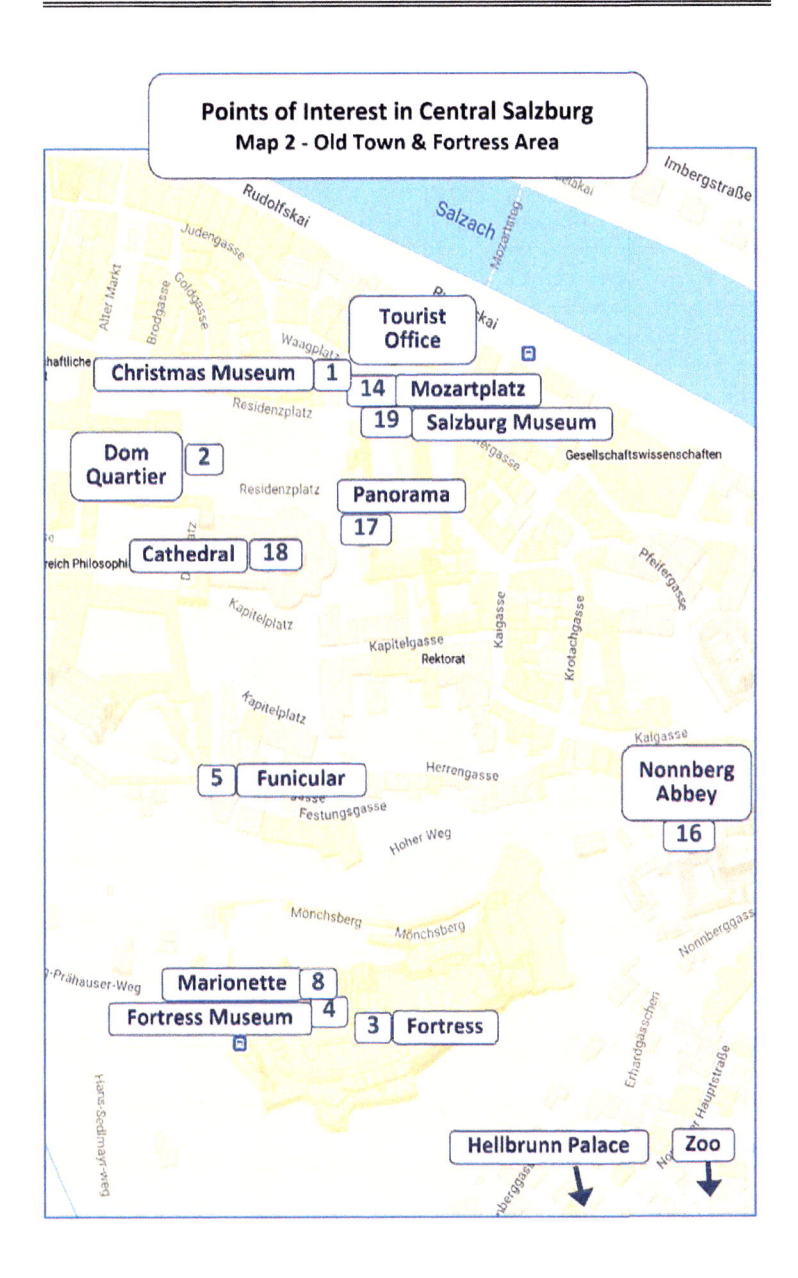

Points of Interest in Central Salzburg
Map 2 - Old Town & Fortress Area

- Christmas Museum — 1
- 14 Mozartplatz
- Tourist Office
- 19 Salzburg Museum
- Dom Quartier — 2
- Panorama — 17
- Cathedral — 18
- 5 Funicular
- Nonnberg Abbey — 16
- Marionette — 8
- Fortress Museum — 4
- 3 Fortress
- Hellbrunn Palace
- Zoo

Salzburg Points of Interest

Attractions cited with "n/a" for Map # are outside of the historical center of Salzburg.

Destination	Map #	Area of Town
Christmas Museum	1	Old Town
DomQuartier (Palace)	2	Old Town
Fortress Hohensalzburg	3	Old Town
Fortress Museum	4	Old Town
Funicular	5	Old Town
Getreidegasse Street	6	Old Town
Hellbrunn Palace	n/a	South of Town
Karajan Sq & Horse Pond	7	Old Town
Marionette Museum	8	Old Town
Mirabell Gardens	9	New Town
Mirabell Palace	10	New Town
Modern Art Museum	11	Old Town
Mozart's Birthplace	12	Old Town
Mozart Residence	13	New Town
MozartPlatz	14	Old Town
Natural History Museum	15	Old Town
Nonnberg Abbey	16	Old Town

Salzburg Points of Interest		
Attractions cited with "n/a" for Map # are outside of the historical center of Salzburg.		
Destination	**Map #**	**Area of Town**
Panorama Museum	17	Old Town
Salzburg Cathedral	18	Old Town
Salzburg Museum	19	Old Town
Salzburg Zoo	n/a	South of Town
Toy Museum	20	Old Town

1-Christmas Museum / Salzburger Weihnachtsmuseum:

Description: This is a small museum which would be easy to miss if you weren't looking for it. Located over a café next to Mozartplatz, this museum provides a delightful display of Christmas traditions, old advent calendars, nativity scenes, dioramas, historical Christmas cards, and more.

It doesn't take long to see the exhibits, but they are well done and worth a visit while exploring Salzburg's Old Town.

Hours: Hours and days open vary by the season. The museum is closed during February and early March. When open, typical hours are 10am to 6pm except Sunday.

Address: Mozartplatz 2, A-5020 Salzburg.

Website: **www.Salzburger-Weihnachtsmuseum.at**

~ ~ ~ ~ ~

2- DomQuartier & Salzburg Palace

Description: This is a beautiful Baroque palace which now houses multiple museums. Portions of this complex date to the 12th century with most of the "newer" structures added in the early 17th century. From the outside, the buildings appear plain. It is when you enter and explore the numerous chambers and galleries that the structure's ornate qualities become apparent.

One of many beautiful rooms in the DomQuartier / Salzburg Palace

Try to allow for at least two hours to explore the main areas of this complex. This includes:
- Numerous state rooms
- The Residenz Gallery – focus is on European paintings.
- Cathedral Museum
- St. Peter's Museum
- Long Gallery – a former painting gallery of archbishops.

Address: Residenzplatz 1, 5020 Salzburg. In the center of the historic district, adjacent to the large Residenzplatz plaza.

Hours: 10am to 5pm – closed Dec 24.

Cost: Included in the Salzburg card or €13 for adults, youth rate is €8, seniors are €10. (All rates subject to change)

Website: www.DomQuartier.at

3 – Fortress Hohensalzburg / Festung Hohensalzburg:

Description: If you visit only one of Salzburg's attractions, this should be it. This massive fortress is perched above the city and provides incredible, photo-worthy, views in every direction. These viewpoints alone show how this location is a perfect site to watch over the area below and guard against intruders.

Fortress Hohensalzburg

This is the largest preserved castle in central Europe. Built in the 11th century, it is a massive complex of fortress, palace, and museums. Its size it is over 800 feet in length (250 meters) and nearly 500 feet wide (150 meters). With nearly one million visitors each year, this is one of Austria's top attractions.

The original structure was partially of wood. It was expanded and fortified in the 15th century and again in the 17th century to include the outer walls and towers which are some of the more prominent features.

The entire complex was refurbished late in the 19th century and the funicular railway up to it was opened. During WWI it was used to hold Italian prisoners of war.

Today, visitors may explore most of the grounds and museums. Some attractions require a more expensive pass than the basic one. (See next page). Take time to grab a meal and enjoy the expansive courtyard.

What Is Here:
- Castle grounds, courtyards, and fortress complex.
- Fortress museum
- Marionette museum
- Princely Chambers
- Panorama tour – an extensive set of dioramas which take you deep into the castle.
- Saint-George's Church
- Regiment Museum
- Armoury
- Magic Theater
- Funicular
- Café
- Restrooms and shops.

> **If you have a Salzburg Pass, admission is free, including the funicular.**

Getting Here: You have two very different ways of traveling to the fortress complex and both are fun. You may mix-and-match the options of: (a) a funicular which starts out of the Old Town area below and/or (b) a scenic 20-minute walk which has great views, but some stamina is required.

Tickets: There is a mix of ticket options which can be confusing. A big difference in the ticket groupings is if you prefer to ride the funicular up to the castle or take the scenic footpath. These tickets fall into the groupings of **"Basic"** or **"All-Inclusive."** The following table outlines what is included in each pass. If you have a Salzburg Pass, no further ticket purchase is necessary.

Fortress Hohensalzburg Pass Options			
	Basic Pass		**All-Inclusive Pass**	
Feature	Take Pathway Up	Take Funicular	Pathway Up	Funicular
Funicular Up		♦		♦
Funicular Down	♦	♦	♦	♦
Castle Area	♦	♦	♦	♦
Museums	♦	♦	♦	♦
Princely Chambers			♦	♦
Magic Theater			♦	♦
Adult Rate	€10,30	€13,30	€12,60	€16,60
Child Rate	€5,90	€7,60	€7,20	€9,50

Website: **www.Salzburg-Burgen.at** (Then select Festung Hohensalzburg)

4 – Fortress Museum / Festungsmuseum

Description: Once you enter the Hohensalzburg Fortress grounds, you can view several attractions including the Fortress Museum. The museum documents the history and evolution of Fortress Hohensalzburg. Many exhibits showcase life in the fortress along with archaeological discoveries dating to Roman times. There is an expansive set of weapons, armor, and torture devices on display.

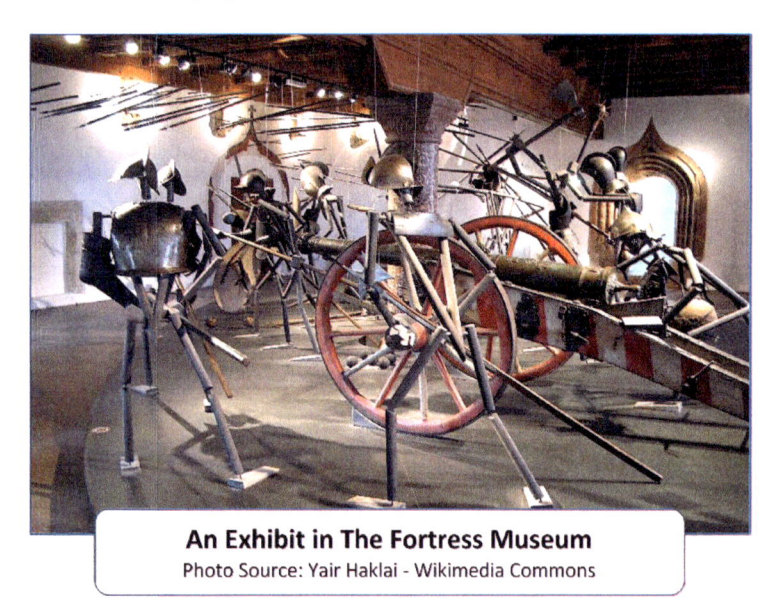

An Exhibit in The Fortress Museum
Photo Source: Yair Haklai - Wikimedia Commons

Hours: Varies by the season. The most common hours are from 9:30am to 5pm. During summer, it stays open until 7pm.

Cost: There is no additional fee once you have purchased a pass to the fortress grounds.

Website: www.SalzburgMuseum.at (Then look for the link on the left of the page to the Fortress Museum.)

5 – Funicular / FestungsBahn:

Description: The funicular up to the fortress, also referred to as the Fortress Railway, is a completely enjoyable way to travel uphill to begin your explorations in the Fortress and its museums.

   This funicular service has been operating since 1892, making it Austria's oldest active funicular. The cars and track you now ride on are far more modern than the original versions and were modernized in 2011. This ride takes only a minute, but even for a short ride, it is an enjoyable experience. The cars hold up to 55 people and reservations are not required, nor is there a reservation system.

To get to the bottom station, head toward Kapitelplatz adjacent to the cathedral in Old Town. From there, the funicular and station are clearly visible.

Cost: There is no additional fee once you have purchased a pass to the fortress grounds.

Website: www.5schaetze.at (Then look for the link to the Fortress Railway.)

6– Grain Alley / Getreidegasse Street & Area:

Description: It should come as no surprise, given the popularity of Salzburg, that there is some tremendous shopping and browsing here. Ground zero for enjoyable shopping for tourist items,

Getreidegasse
Popular Old Town (Altstadt) shopping lane.
Photo Source: J. Franganillo - Wikimedia Commons

upscale garments, jewelry, and much more, is along the quarter-mile long street with the long name of Getreidegasse, also known as Grain Alley.

Salzburg's Altstadt (Old Town) is something of a maze and it would be easy to completely miss this popular section of town if you weren't looking for it. This pedestrian street stretches east-west, parallel to the river and one block in. A key landmark to look for, especially if you need directions to this shopping mecca, is to ask for Mozart's Birthplace. This historical treasure sits along this lane.

This pedestrian shopping haven is more than the Getreidegasse, the connecting lanes such as Kanzlmarkt are every bit as lively.

Hellbrunn Palace / Schloss Hellbrunn:[13]

Description: A beautiful mansion and grounds which are definitely worth visiting. There is enough here for several hours of exploration.

The Hellbrunn Palace was built in 1613, making it over 400 years old. Curiously, given that the palace was built to be a day retreat during the summer months, there are no bedrooms here. The building was made in Renaissance style, popular in Italy at this time, and the decorations are very ornate. The Folklore Museum is included in the attractions here.

In addition to the palace, a popular and fun feature are the Trick Fountains. There are many fountains, small and large,

---

[13] *Sound of Music* and **Hellbrunn Palace:** Many individuals confuse this palace with Villa Trapp, the real home of the Trapp family. They are not the same. This palace was used for several scenes in the movie, but it is not the Trapp home. Villa Trapp is much closer to central Salzburg and is <u>not</u> a noteworthy stop. It is not currently open to tours. Villa Trapp had been an active inn until recently.

throughout the grounds. Many were built to be surprises to guests such as a fountain coming out of the seat of an outdoor chair. These fountains only operate from April to early November.

Hellbrunn Palace

There are large formal gardens adjacent to the palace, giving it an enjoyable setting. In addition, an expansive open green space, the Hellbrunner Park, gives visitors a great area to relax.

The Salzburg Zoo is adjacent to the palace grounds and the two attractions can easily be combined into a day trip. The walk between the two is only five minutes.

Getting Here: The palace is 2 ½ miles south of central Salzburg. It may be reached by car, Hop-On Bus, or bicycle. If you choose to bring a car, parking is an extra fee. The Hop-On Bus stops directly outside of the palace entrance.

Hours: Varies by the season and not open in winter months. Opening time from April 1 to Nov 1 is 9:30am. Closing time is 5:30pm in the late fall, and open until 7pm in summer.

Cost: If you have purchased a Salzburg Card, there is no additional fee. Adult fare is €13.50 (as of summer-2022) and child rate is €6.

Website: www.Hellbrunn.at

7 – Karajan Square & Horse Pond / Herbert von Karajan-Platz:

Description: Tucked away from the primary area of Old Town is a small plaza in a dramatic setting. This square is backed up to the rocky cliff face which frames much of Salzburg's historic area. This set of cliffs are the **Mönchsberg Cliffs** and the decorative "Sigmunds Gate" tunnel portal. If you are adventurous, you may take a trail to the upper areas and follow it to the fortress.

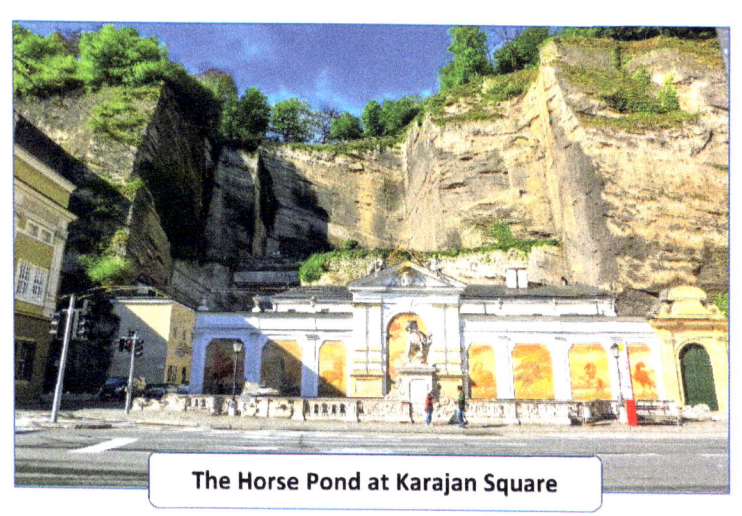

The Horse Pond at Karajan Square

At the base of these cliffs are two interesting features. The ornate **Horse Pond** was crafted in 1603 and used as a place to wash parade horses. The statue in the center is called the "Horse Tamer."

Easily missed is a tunnel into the cliffside, the Siegmundstor. You may walk through it, but be advised that it is busy, narrow, noisy, and potentially dangerous. This tunnel is the oldest highway tunnel in Austria, built in 1640.

Getting Here: The plaza and Horse Pond are a few blocks west from the Cathedral or just two blocks south of the shopping street Getreidegasse which was described earlier in this section. It is also a stop on the Hop-On bus.

Address: Herbert-von-Karajan-Plata 11, 5020 Salzburg.

8- Marionette Museum / Marionetten Museum:

Description: A fun component of a visit to the Fortress Hohensalzburg, is stopping in to view the small Marionette Museum. This unique museum is in the area of the fortress known as the Prince's Basement. The marionettes and puppets on display are very ornate and are far from simple toys.

It takes less than thirty minutes to view this fun collection so, while you are exploring the fortress, consider stopping in. There are dioramas and marionettes dedicated to the music of Mozart among the displays.

This destination is also referred to as "The World of Marionettes."

Hours: Same as the fortress.

Cost: No additional fee. It is included in the Fortress entrance pass.

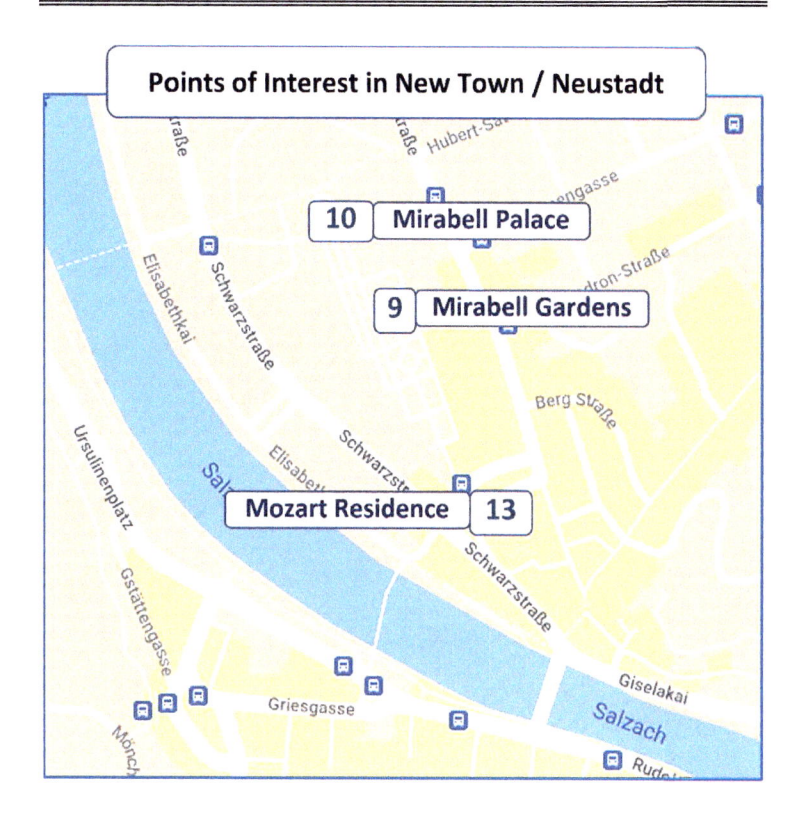

9 - Mirabell Gardens / Mirabellgarten:

Description: There are a small number of notable sights in the Neustadt area and the Mirabell Gardens with the adjoining palace are at the top of the list. This popular formal garden area was first laid out in the 17th century. Around the gardens are eight statues of ancient gods and four baroque statues symbolizing the elements of water. At the heart of the gardens is the Pegasus fountain. There is also an enjoyable dwarf garden.

These gardens are free to stroll through and no pass is needed.

A Starting-Point Guide

Mirabell Gardens in Neustadt
Photo Source: Raimond Spekking - Wikimedia Commons

10- Mirabell Palace / Schloss Mirabell:[14]

Description: This palace, which is adjacent to Mirabell Gardens, is not only an historical treasure, it is listed as a cultural heritage monument.

The focal point within Mirabell Palace is the Marble Hall, a former ballroom of the Prince Archbishop in the early 17th century. This hall is not large and only takes a minute or two to visit.

Mirabell Palace / Schloss Mirabell

Today, the Marble Hall is open to regular concerts and numerous weddings. This is a cultural highlight of a visit to Salzburg and, if your schedule allows, try to book tickets to one of the evening concerts. As you may expect, much of the music for these events focuses on Mozart and Vivaldi, who both have resided in Salzburg.

---

[14] **Mirabell Name**: This name comes from Italian and roughly translates to "Admirable Beauty."

Getting Here: In the heart of Salzburg's New Town (Neustadt) district. The street address is Mirabellplatz 4, 5020 Salzburg. This is a Hop-On bus stop.

Hours: The Marbel Hall is open every day except Sunday. Hours vary by the day. Monday, Wednesday, and Thursday normal hours are 8am to 4pm. On Tuesday and Friday, it is only open in the afternoon from 1pm to 4pm. This palace is the location for many notable events and these can impact the opening hours.

Cost: There is no charge to visit the palace and Marbel Hall.

Websites: **www.Salzburg.info** Then go to the section labeled "top 10 sights." Also, to view the concert schedule, go to **www.Salzburg-Palace-Concerts.com**.

11-Modern Art Museum / Museum der Moderne Salzburg Mönchsberg:

Description: There are two locales for Salzburg's Modern Art Museum. The more popular locale is on a rise overlooking the river and much of historic Salzburg. Come here for the art, the views, a great café, and an impressive building. The site on the Mönchsberg Hill has nearly 25,000 sq feet (2,300 sq meters) of displays spread across four floors.

> **Come for the views!**
>
> The views of Salzburg from this museum and its café are superb. Be sure to bring a camera.

There are over 50,000 works in the collection including art, photography, and sculptures.

The museum has a café with one of the best views to be found of Salzburg. Take time to enjoy the outdoor portion of the café, view the river, and both Neustadt and Aldstadt below you.

Modern Art Museum Mönchsberg
Photo Source: Andreas Praefcke - Wikimedia Commons

Getting Here: The museum sits on a hill directly across the river from Mirabell Gardens. It is outside the primary historic center of Altstadt and is roughly a 15- to 20-minute walk northwest from the heart of Old Town. Once you reach the base, there is a modern store front labeled "Museum der Moderne." This storefront leads you to an elevator which takes you up into the museum.

Address of the elevator: Gstättengasse 13, 5020 Salzburg.

Hours: Tuesday to Sunday 10am to 6pm. Closed Monday except during the summer festival.

Cost: If you have purchased a Salzburg Card, there is no additional fee. Adult fare is €15, Seniors €12, and children 6 to 14 €8,80. (Rates are as of summer-2022 and subject to change.)

Website: **www.MuseumDerModerne.at**

12-Mozart's Birthplace / Mozart's Geburtshaus:

Description: Sitting on the popular shopping street Getreidegasse in Old Town is a bright yellow building which is famous for being Mozart's birthplace.

It would be easy, given his fame, to assume the entire building had belonged to the Mozart's family. In actuality, they only occupied one modest apartment on the third floor. This apartment, and an adjoining area, is now a small museum.

Visiting here provides an excellent insight into both Mozart and what life was like for many families here in the 18th century. Mozart was the seventh child of Leopold & Anna Maria Mozart, so there were quite a few people living in this space.

Mozart's Birthplace
Photo Source:
A. Stiasny - Wikimedia Commons

The family lived here from 1747 until 1773. Wolfgang Amadeus Mozart was born in 1756. In 1773 they moved across the river to the Mozart Residence in Neustadt, near the Mirabell Gardens and Palace.

Address: Getreidegasse 9, 5020 Salzburg

Hours: Every day except some holidays from 9am to 5:30pm.

Cost: Included in the Salzburg Card. Adult fare is €12 and children 6 to 14 €5. A combination ticket which includes the Mozart Residence is available. The adult rate for this combination is €18,50. (Rates are as of summer-2022 and subject to change.)

Website: www.Mozarteum.at

13-Mozart's Residence / Mozart-Wohnhaus:

Description: This is one of two notable locales where Mozart lived with his family. They moved here from the apartment across the river in Altstadt as it was too small for their needs.

Mozart's Salzburg Residence in New Town
Photo Source: Google Earth

    The residence is in a pleasant setting next to a small park and very close to Mirabell Gardens. A visit to this residence can easily be combined with Mirabell Gardens and Palace. There are several restaurants nearby, including one in the same building as the Mozart Residence.

The museum here includes many of his instruments and documents. There are also presentations on the home and life here.

Address: Makartplatz 8, 5020 Salzburg

Hours: Every day except some holidays from 9am to 5:30pm.

Cost: Included in the Salzburg Card. Adult fare is €12 and children 6 to 14 €5. A combination ticket which includes the Mozart Birthplace is available. The adult rate for this combination is €18,50. (Rates are as of summer-2022 and subject to change.)

Website: www.Mozarteum.at (This website covers both the Mozart Birthplace and Mozart's Salzburg Residence).

14-Mozart Square / Mozartplatz:

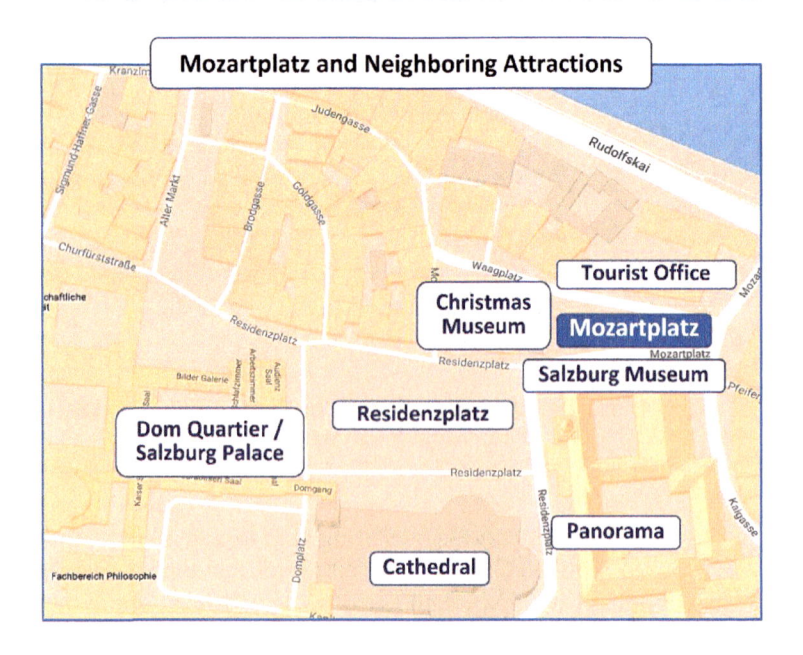

Description: This square in Salzburg's Old Town is an excellent place to begin explorations of the city. In the middle of the square is a statue of Wolfgang Amadeus Mozart which was crafted in 1841. Underneath the statue a Roman mosaic has been discovered and a copy of this may be seen here.

If you come to Salzburg during Christmas, Salzburg Advent or Christkindlmarkt, many activities and booths will be found here.

In the immediate vicinity of this plaza are the:

- Tourist Office
- Christmas Museum
- Residenzplatz – a large open square.
- Salzburg Museum
- Residenz Palace
- Panorama Museum
- Several shops and stores

Address: Mozartplatz, 5020 Salzburg

Photo Source: Michielverbeek - Wikipedia

~ ~ ~ ~ ~ ~

15- Museum of Natural History / Haus der Natur:

Description: For starters, this museum is huge. With nearly 75,000 sq ft of exhibit space (7,000 sq meters), this museum rivals those in much larger cities.

Salzburg's Haus der Natur / Natural History Museum
Photo Source: Google Maps

The museum covers a broad spectrum of science and nature including:
- Aquarium and Reptile Zoo
- A Science Center
- Journey into the Human Body
- Primeval Times and Dinosaurs
- The Universe
- World of Oceans
- The Ice Age....and many other topics.

A full-service café with outdoor seating is on site.

Address: Museumspl 5, 5020 Salzburg. This is located at the outer edge of Old Town, and roughly across the river from the Mozart Residence. The Salzburg Modern Art Museum is less than one block south from here. The Salzburg Hop-On bus stops here.

Hours: Every day except some holidays from 9am to 5pm.

Cost: Included in the Salzburg Card., or adult fare is €9,50 and the child rate is €7.

Website: **www.HausDerNatur.at**

16- Nonnberg Abbey / Stift Nonnberg:

Description: For individuals who enjoy the movie *The Sound of Music*, it is a fun fact to know this abbey is where the story begins. This is an active Benedictine abbey with regular services and the nuns do sing Gregorian songs every morning.

Nonnberg Abbey

This is not a tourist attraction in the traditional sense, but you may visit the interior which is beautiful. While it is early for most of us, if you can come at 6:45am, you will be able to hear the nuns sing.

Among the treasures here is a crucifix dating to the 14th century and there are wall paintings which were done in the 12th century.

Address: Nonnberggasse 2, 5020 Salzburg. This abbey sits on a rise above Old Town and is a short climb up narrow lanes to reach it.

Hours: The church is open from 6:30am to 6pm most days. Vespers, which are sung, occur weekdays at 5:15pm.

Cost: There is no fee to visit this church.

Website: www.Nonnberg.at

17- Panorama Museum:

Description: Located on Residence Square, this is a very well-done depiction of Salzburg as it was in 1829. The primary exhibit is a 360 degree, highly detailed, circular painting. This work has been highly praised for its historical accuracy.

In addition to the panorama, other dioramas and paintings are available for viewing. Total time to visit is short and it is easy to add this unique exhibit in with other explorations of Old Town Salzburg.

Address: Residenzpl 9, 5020 Salzburg. This is adjacent to the Residenzplatz and a short walk to Mozartplatz.

Hours: 9am to 5pm. Closed on holidays.

Cost: Free if you have a Salzburg Card, otherwise, the adult rate is €4,50 and the child rate is €1,50.

Website: www.SalzburgMuseum.at Then click on the link to "The Panorama" in the left side navigation.

18- Salzburg Cathedral / Dom zu Salzburg:

Salzburg Cathedral

Description: Salzburg is rich in beautiful and historic structures and this large cathedral, which sits in the center of the historic district, is at the top of the list.

The history of this church dates to 774. The current structure was rebuilt in the Baroque style in the 17th century. This large building sits on top of earlier Roman ruins. Over the years, it has had numerous major fires causing it to be fully rebuilt three different times.

This church was designated a UNESCO World Heritage Site in 1997.

In addition to the overall beauty of the interior, there are several components which are worth noting and visiting:

- The baptismal font in which Wolfgang Amadeus Mozart was baptized is near the entrance.
- Four large statues at the front represent apostles Peter and Paul and two patron saints Virgil and Rupert. Rupert is the patron saint of Salzburg.
- Inside, the beautiful dome is 232 feet high (71 meters).
- The frescoes are from scenes of the Old Testimate.
- There is an ancient crypt and you can see parts of the first buildings.

Address: Domplatz 1a, 5020 Salzburg. The Domplatz plaza is adjacent to both the Salzburg Palace (DomQuartier) and Residenzplatz.

Hours: Monday to Saturday, it is open from 8am until 5pm and sometimes until 6pm. Sunday and holidays, the cathedral is not open for visits until 1pm.

Cost: Unlike most churches, there is a modest conservation fee to tour this cathedral. Several options are available:

- Entrance fee for adults is €5 and free for children up to 18.
- Rental of an audio guide is €3.
- Guided Tour: €5 for adult. (Private tours are available for a minimum of €70.
- Lunchtime music event is €6.

Website: www.Salzburger-dom.at

19- Salzburg Museum – New Residence:

Description: The Salzburg Museum is a network of museums. The one which is typically thought of as the primary Salzburg Museum has the more complete name of Salzburg Museum-Neue Residenz (New Residence). Using this name helps ensure you are heading to the desired locale.

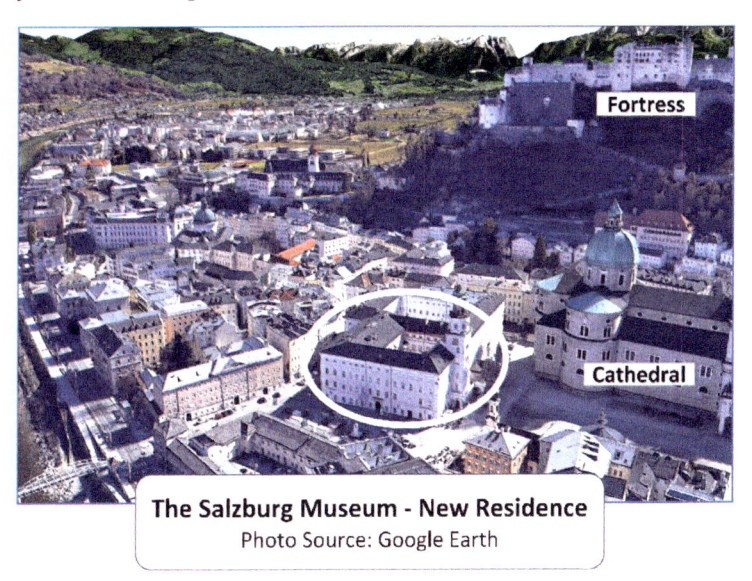

The Salzburg Museum - New Residence
Photo Source: Google Earth

This is a comprehensive history and culture museum of Salzburg and Austria. One of the more popular areas is titled "Myths of Salzburg." The collections are in the building known as "Neue Residence," a former palace. This helps distinguish it from what is referred to as the Salzburg Palace or Old Residence.

Address: Mozartplatz 1, 5010 Salzburg. The main entrance faces the Mozartplatz, across from the Tourist Office.

Hours: Tuesday – Sunday 9am to 5pm. Closed on Monday.

Cost: Included in the Salzburg Card, or adult €9 and children are €3.

Website: www.SalzburgMuseum.at The Salzburg Museum is a collection of several entities including the Salzburg Museum outlined here, Fortress Museum, Toy Museum, and others. This website outlines each of these destinations.

Salzburg Zoo / Salzburg Zoo Hellbrunn:

Description: At first, it would be easy to dismiss this as "just another small city zoo." In a word, don't. The setting for this 34-acre (14 hectare) zoo is unique and spectacular. There are rocky outcroppings and passages to explore, intriguing forest trails, and formal gardens. Views here of the mountains to the south are near-perfect.

There are 1,500 animals here and often are together as this zoo takes the approach to not separate species when possible. One result of this is a feeling of openness as you explore the grounds.

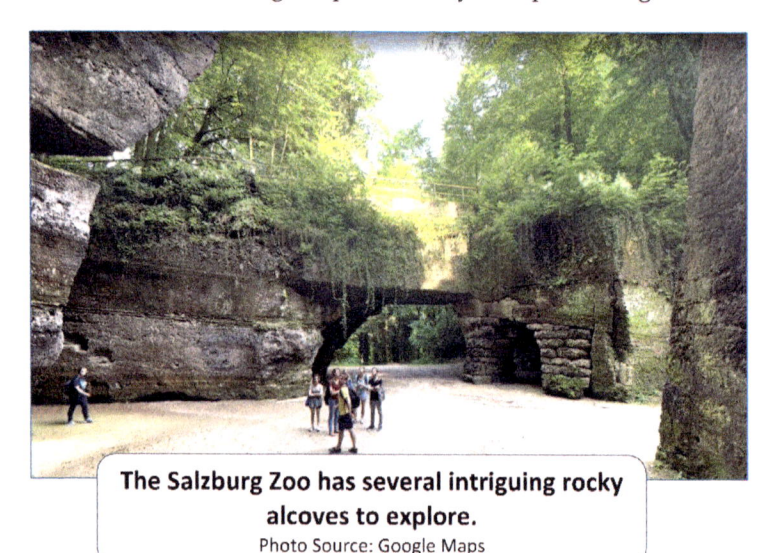

The Salzburg Zoo has several intriguing rocky alcoves to explore.
Photo Source: Google Maps

Address: Zoo Salzburg, Hellbrunner Strasse 60, 5081 Anif, Austria.

Getting Here: The zoo is adjacent to the Hellbrunn Palace and the zoo parking is immediately south of the palace gardens. This complex is slightly over 2 miles south of central Salzburg. It is easy to park at the zoo and walk over to the palace if you wish to combine attractions. The Hop-On bus does stop here. If you wish to take a bus from central Strasbourg, catch line 25.

Hours: Vary by the season. During the popular spring, summer, and fall, typical hours are 9am to 6pm. Hours are shorter in the winter. Check the website for exact hours for the timeframe you will be here

Cost: Included in the Salzburg Card or adult fare is €12,50 and child fare are €8. All fares are subject to change.

Website: www.Salzburg-Zoo.at

20 – Toy Museum / Spielzeug Museum:

Description: This is a specialty museum on the edge of Salzburg's historic district. The museum boasts a large collection of antique toys. For children, there are many interactive and hands-on exhibits such as a maze, a fun slide, and racecar driving experience.

Address: Bürgerspitalgasse 2, 5020 Salzburg, Austria. This location is between the Horse Pond and the Modern Art Museum. This is a 10-minute walk to the Cathedral area.

Hours: Tuesday to Sunday 9am to 5pm. Closed on Monday.

Cost: Included in the Salzburg Card or adult fare is €5 and child fare are €2. All fares are subject to change.

Website: www.Spielzeugmuseum.at

~ ~ ~ ~ ~ ~

8: Beer/Bier Houses & Gardens

Beer (or "Bier" in German) and the breweries which make it are a central part of the area's culture. Yes, Salzburg has a full array of fine and unique dining, but you are in Austria, next to Bavaria and within walking distance of beer gardens from almost any point in Salzburg. So, well, enjoy some local beer and do so in a lively setting.

For a bit of clarification, in its purest definition, a "Beer Garden" can be any establishment which serves beer and local dishes and generally does so in an outdoor setting. This guide will focus on the larger and more popular destinations.

When you are in Salzburg, you have the opportunity to visit some impressive beer gardens, several breweries, take beer tours, or even walk "The Beer Route."

For some added fun, consider purchasing some local folk wear including lederhosen and dirndl dresses. There are several shops in the heart of Altstadt. Just head to the popular

Beer Route

Scan the code below to obtain an interactive map of Salzburg's beer walk.

Beer Houses & Gardens

shopping street Getreidegasse or the adjoining Rathausplatz, (near Mozart's birthplace) for starters.

Beer/Bier Gardens and Bier Houses:

A dozen of the cities more noted beer houses are outlined here. This is far from being a complete list. Each of these locales provide a fun experience with ample local flavor and cuisine.

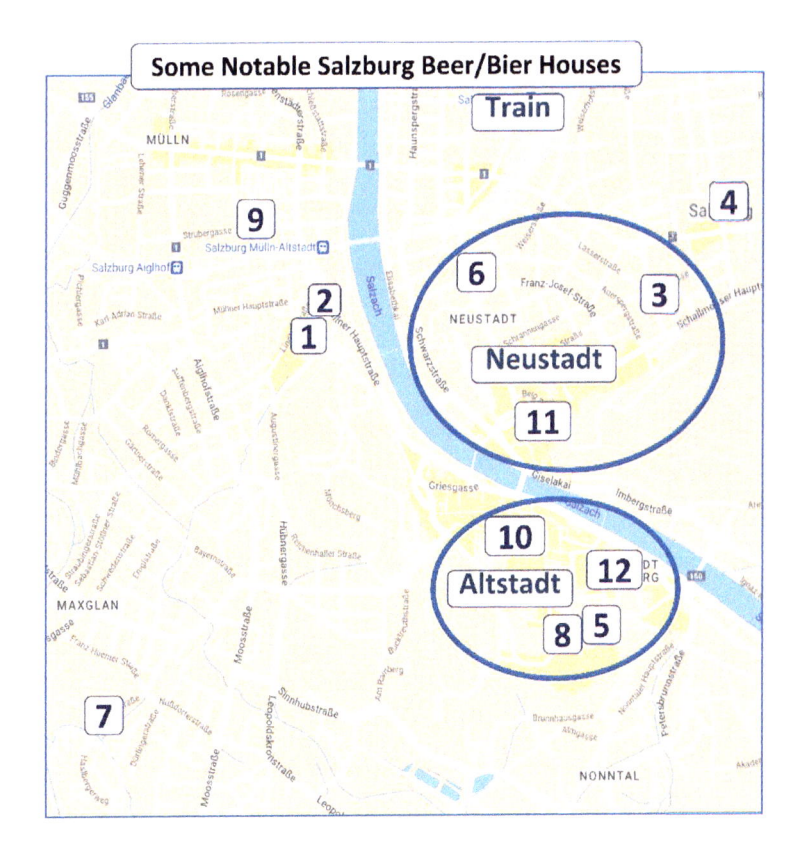

Some Notable Salzburg Beer/Bier Houses

Suggested Beer Gardens in or near central Salzburg

(All selected locations provide area cuisine)

Map #	Name & Details	
1	**Augistiner bräu – Kloster Mülln**	
	Area:	1 mile north of Alstadt
	Address:	Lindhofstraße 7
	Website:	www.Augustinerbier.at
2	**Augustiner Braugasthof Krimpelstätter**	
	Area:	1 mile north of Alstadt
	Address:	Müllner Haupstraße 31
	Website:	www.Krimpelstaetter.at
3	**Die Weisse**	
	Area:	Neustadt – 10-minute walk east from Mirabell Gardens.
	Address:	Rupertgasse 10
	Website:	www.DieWeisse.at
4	**Fuxn**	
	Area:	Neustadt – ¾ mile east from Mirabell Gardens
	Address:	Vogelweiderstraße 28
	Website:	www.Fuxn.at

Beer Houses & Gardens

Suggested Beer Gardens in or near central Salzburg

(All selected locations provide area cuisine)

Map #	Name & Details	
5	**Pauli Stubm**	
	Area:	Altstadt – below the fortress and tucked away on a side street.
	Address:	Herrengasse 16
	Website:	www.Paul-Staube.at
6	**PitterKeller & PitterGarten**	
	Area:	Neustadt – 1 block north from Mirabell Palace
	Address:	Rainerstrasse 6 Ecke
	Website:	www.Imlauer.com/Pitterkeller
7	**Stiegl-Brauwelt**	
	Area:	West of Alstadt near the airport.
	Address:	Bräuhausstraße 9
	Website:	www.Brauwelt.at
8	**Stiegl-Keller**	
	Area:	Altstadt – below the fortress 1 block east of the funicular.
	Address:	Festungsgasse 10
	Website:	www.Restaurant-Stieglkeller.at

Suggested Beer Gardens in or near central Salzburg

(All selected locations provide area cuisine)

Map #	Name & Details	
9	**Trumerei Restaurant & Biershop**	
	Area:	North of Alstadt – across the river from the train station.
	Address:	Strubergasse 26
	Website:	www.Trumeri.at
10	**Zipfer Bierhaus**	
	Area:	Alstadt – in the heart of the historic district.
	Address:	Universitätsplatz 19
	Website:	www.Zipfer-Bierhaus.com
11	**Zum Fidelen Affen**	
	Area:	Neustadt – 1 block south of Mirabell Gardens.
	Address:	Priesterhausgasse 8
	Website:	
12	**Zum Zirkelwirt**	
	Area:	Altstadt – 2 blocks east from the cathedral.
	Address:	Pfeifergasse 14
	Website:	www.ZumZirkelwirt.at

9: Salt Mines Near Salzburg

Explore the area's White Gold

The Salzach River which runs through Salzburg is named after salt. This river had been an important shipping route for Salt and there are several salt mines near Salzburg.

Salt has often been referred to as white gold and has been mined in the region for thousands of years when it was harvested by early Celtic tribes. Salt was used to preserve food as there was no refrigeration and the salt mined here was shipped by river throughout central Europe.

During WWII, the Nazis used these mines to hide art and other treasures taken from museums. Portions of the movie *Monuments Men* was filmed here in the area's salt caves.

When you visit Salzburg, consider visiting one of these mines. Some mines are located on the Salzach River such as the Berchtesgaden Salt Mines which are a short 30-minute trip south from central Salzburg. Tours are available into the mines; some include boat tours. Almost every mine tour includes a mine train ride, and you can expect to put on some miner's clothing which adds some fun to the experience.

Caution:
If you don't like dark spaces with minimal head room, these tours may not be right for you.

An often-unexpected aspect of visiting these mines is many are set into beautiful mountain areas. Consider making it a day to not only tour one of the mines, but explore the mountains and take a short hike as well.

If you purchase one of the available Salzburg area travel cards, see chapter 5, many of these tours are included and will either be free or discounted.

Ride a small train deep into the salt mines at Berchtesgaden.
Photo Source: Colin Smith - Wikimedia Commons

This chapter outlines three popular salt mines which are easy excursions from Salzburg. These are not the only popular mines in Austria, but others are further afield such as in Hallstatt. Structured tours are available to most of these destinations, and several are listed near the end of this chapter.

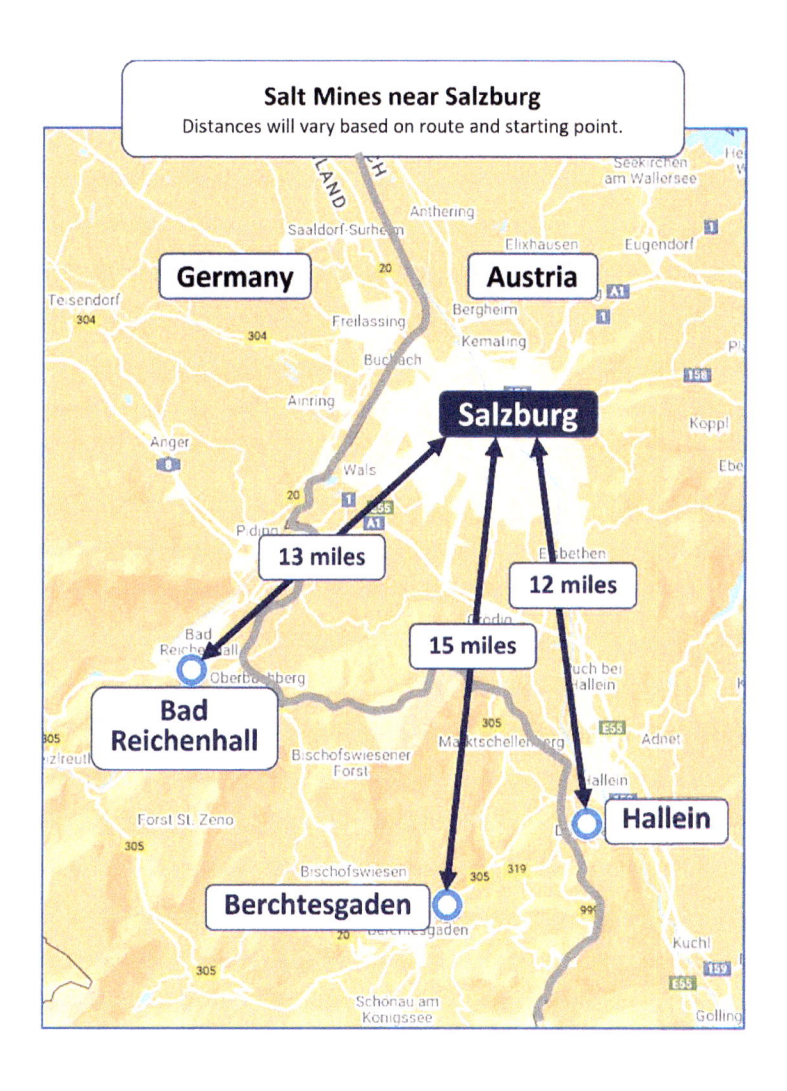

Salt Mines Near Salzburg

Salt Mines near Salzburg
Distances will vary based on route and starting point.

- Bad Reichenhall — 13 miles
- Berchtesgaden — 15 miles
- Hallein — 12 miles

Salt Mines near Salzburg:

Hallein Salt Mine / Salzwelten Salzburg: This is one of the world's oldest salt mines and the easiest to reach from central Salzburg. Visitors take a train ride deep into the mountain. Once inside the mines, additional travel modes include a raft ride across an underground lake and the fun of shooshing down steep slides even further into the complex.

> **Limited Mobility**
>
> The mine tours are **not** available for individuals in wheelchairs.

This mine now has 9 miles (12km) of tunnels open and this spans 21 underground levels. In its prime, there had been 40 miles of tunnels.

To visit the mines, you must join a tour as individual explorations are not allowed. Tours take 90-minutes and you must be able to walk slightly over ½ mile (1 kilometer). One option available is hiring a private tour guide. Advance reservations are highly recommended.

This cave system is open all year except some holidays. Come early during the summer season as this is a popular attraction.

- **Address:** Ramsaustraße 3, 5422 Bad Dürnberg, Austria. This mine complex is in the hills above the town of Hallein. Distance to central Hallein is roughly 3 miles.

- **How to Get Here:** By car, this is a 25–30-minute drive from central Salzburg. A train-bus combo also works well. Take the train to Hallein from Salzburg then there is a bus every 30 minutes up to the mine. Another option is to take one of the many group or private tours from Salzburg.

- **Website**: www.Salzwelten.at Then click on the link to locations to view info on the Hallein area mine. This is listed as the Salzburg mine. Use this website to determine current cost as there are several price points and packages available.

Salt Mine Berchtesgaden: Even before you enter the mine complex, it soon becomes apparent that this mine and town are in a postcard-perfect setting. This is located in the Bavarian hills and the town adjacent to the mine and the views in every direction are beautiful.

Berchtesgaden, Germany

This large mine dates to the 12th century with active salt harvesting beginning in the 16th century. Visitors to this mine dress up in miner's clothing and take a train deep underground. In addition to the underground lake and slides, there is also an enjoyable laser light show. The one-hour tours require a guide and each visitor is given an audio guide available in multiple languages. Like other salt caves, visitors with limited mobility should not attempt to take the tours.

Visiting here can, and perhaps should, be a full day experience. It is near the noted Eagle's Nest retreat of Adolph Hitler and the delightful town of Berchtesgaden. Several available tours combine this mine with the Eagle's Nest.

- **Address:** Salzburger Straße 24, 83471 Berchtesgaden, Germany. The mines are a short distance north of the town and its train station.

- **How to Get Here:** This mine is in Germany and easy to reach by car, train, or bus from Salzburg. By car, this is a 30-minute drive from central Salzburg. Bus travel is very easy. Take bus 840 from Salzburg which departs around every 30 to 45 minutes and the buses stop at the salt works. If you choose to take the train, it is a 20-minute walk from the Berchtesgaden train station to the mines.

- **Website**: **www.Salzbergwerk.de**.

~ ~ ~ ~ ~ ~

Old Salt Works /Alte Saline: Located roughly 13 miles southwest from Salzburg is the Old Salt Works (Alte Saline), a mine which is promoted as "The most beautiful Old Salt Works in the world."

Entrance to the Old Salt Works / Alte Saline
Photo Source: Beatrice - Wikimedia Commons

It is unusual for a mining operation to have buildings which are listed as archeological monuments. The building was done under the orders of King Ludwig as one of his many projects to enhance the image of Bavaria. The facility is noted for innovative components such as a brine pipeline and tunnel system.

Visitors are treated to a tour of the salt mine and salt works. There are also healing thermal springs. The guided tour takes one hour and includes numerous steps. Tours are typically in German with an English language pamphlet to help.

- Address: Alte Saline 9, D-83435 Bad Reichehall, Germany. This mine and museum are close to the center of town making it easy to combine a visit to the mine with exploration of this pleasant community.

- How to Get Here: This mine is in Germany, immediately next to the border with Austria. You have the choice of taking the bus, train, or driving. A drive is less than 30 minutes. The bus from central Salzburg takes only 35 minutes plus a short walk to the mine. If you take the train, a change of trains is required, and total travel time is under 50 minutes. Look at www.rome2Rio.com to compare options and obtain exact travel schedules.

- Website: **www.Alte-Saline.de**.

Salt Mine Tours from Salzburg:

An easy way to visit the salt mines around Salzburg is to join one of the many guided tours. These can be either group or private tours. Depending on the destination, the tours will either be a half-day or full day.

Two of the benefits of booking one of these tours is reduction in travel planning and hassle and the likely combining of attractions such as a visit to a salt mine along with a tour of Hitler's Eagle's Nest.

Many tours head to the beautiful town of Hallstatt. This delightful town has one of the region's larger salt mines.

Virtually every tour company listed in chapter 6 of this guide includes one or more tours to salt mines. Examples of some popular tours include:

Salt Mine and *Sound of Music* **Tour:** Combine a visit to the Berchtesgaden salt mine with a tour of filming locations from the *Sound of Music*.
- Duration: Full day, 8 hours. – Large group bus tour.
- Tour Provider: Salzburg Panorama Tours **www.PanoramaTours.com.**

Bavarian Mountain Tour: Explore the Bavarian mountains and area south of Salzburg. The tour includes a visit to the Berchtesgaden salt mine.
- Duration: Full day, 8 hours. Small group, van tour.
- Tour Provider: Bob's Special Tours **www.BobsTours.com.**

Bavarian Alps Tour: This full day tour includes Eagle's Nest, Berchtesgaden salt mine, and drives through the Bavarian countryside.
- Duration: Full day, 9 hours. Large group, bus tour.
- Tour Provider: Salzburg Panorama Tours **www.PanoramaTours.com.**

Berchtesgaden Tour: A short tour which focuses on this popular mine. An easy adventure to fit into any schedule.
- Duration: Half day, 4 hours. Large group, bus tour.
- Tour Provider: Salzburg Panorama Tours **www.PanoramaTours.com.**

~ ~ ~ ~ ~ ~

10: Exciting Day Trips

When exploring the Salzburg region, there is an incredible array of destinations for day trips. It would take

Easy Day Trip Destinations From Salzburg

A Starting-Point Guide

multiple volumes to detail the many beautiful small towns, lakes, mountains, and monuments. This chapter outlines five of the most popular destinations with the goal of providing a variety of experiences across them.

In each case, the locales described here are within a modest commute from Salzburg and an out-and-back journey in one day is easy to do. Unfortunately, few of these locations are easily reached by train, but four of them have good access via area buses. Some destinations, such as Hallstatt, are often included in group tours out of Salzburg.

> **Crowd Caution**
> The beauty of these destinations brings in visitors from all over the world. Expect to encounter crowds.

This guide does not outline the numerous outdoor destinations for hiking, biking, or skiing. This region is rich in adventure potential and separate detailed guidebooks, websites, or apps should be considered. If you are interested in hiking opportunities, check out **www.Kamoot.com** for details on area trails and bike routes

Easy Day Trips from Salzburg		
Destination	**Distance from Salzburg**	**Reachable by Train or Bus?**
Bad Ischl, Austria	33 miles/53km	Bus is best
Eagles Nest, Germany	17 miles/28km	Bus
Hallstatt, Austria	47 miles/75km	Bus is best
Königssee, Germany	17 miles/29km	Bus
Werfen, Austria	29 miles/46km	Train is best

Bad Ischl, Austria:

Nature of Destination: An attractive and popular spa town situated on a river and in an alpine valley.

> **Bad Ischl is nestled in an alpine valley and bisected by the River Traun.**

Description: This town of 14,000 people is an enjoyable retreat to visit, to relax, dine, and do some casual exploration. This has been a destination of royalty since the early 19th century when brine baths were used for medicinal purposes.

There is an enjoyable mix of attractions here, in addition to the town itself, which is a delight to stroll.

- **Kaiser Villa** – This small palace in central Bad Ischl had been the residence of the Habsburgs in the 1800's. Tours of the villa and grounds are available.
- **Kurpark / Kaiser Park**: The grounds around the Kaiser Villa are expansive and include a beer garden, carriage rides, and large grounds to explore.

- **Katrin Cable Car:** Take a 15-minute cable car ride up from town to a beautiful mountain look. There is a café at the top and several hiking trails.
- **Siriuskogl:** Take a walk uphill (steep) from Bad Ischl to a wooden mountain overlook and café. Great views of the town below.
- **FahrzeugMuseum:** An interesting museum with a collection of historic vehicles and airplanes.
- **Parkbad Bad Ischl**: Take advantage of being in a spa town and head to this large pool and waterpark.

> **SalzburgerLand Card**
> This card covers many attractions in towns outside of Salzburg which are not covered by the Salzburg Card.

Location: The town is east of Salzburg in a mountain valley. Driving distance is roughly 33 miles (53km).

How to Get Here: The quickest way to reach the Eagle's Nest is by car. Driving time is around 50 minutes each way. Buses from central Salzburg take a little over an hour. Catch the bus at Salzburg Mirabellplatz. Trains are not recommended as a change of train is required midway and total travel time each way is roughly two hours. By taking a bus or car, you will encounter beautiful scenery all along the route.

Available Tours: Several tours combine a visit to Bad Ischl with Hallstatt, another beautiful town in the vicinity. Most tours are a full 8- or 9-hour day, but you will be able to combine two of Austria's treasures in the process. Check Viator.com or Panorama Tours for options.

Website: **BadIschl.Salzkammergut.at.**

Eagle's Nest, Germany / Kehlsteinhaus:

Nature of Destination: An historical monument, and former retreat for Hitler and Eva Braun, overlooking a beautiful valley and town below.

Description: This historically significant building sits on an overlook at over 6,000 feet (1,800 meters). It was built in 1939 for Hitler's 50th birthday by Martin Bormann. The Eagle's Nest was one of the few buildings in the area to survive bomb raids in WWII as it was a difficult site to hit.

Hitler's Eagle's Nest
Photo Source: Petriukas - Wikipedia

This was a huge construction project and took more than 3,000 people to complete. The project included blasting through the mountain to create a road, numerous tunnels, and a 400-foot-tall elevator shaft.

Today, most visitors choose to take this elevator to the top, although you do have the option of hiking up (a steep hike). Taking the elevator and shuttle bus from the visitor's center requires reservations which must be obtained from the center. If you book a tour, this will be handled in advance for you.

Views at the top are astounding. This is a popular spot and in high season can be quite busy.

Once you are in the area, it is easy to add in a salt mine tour at Berchtesgaden or the beautiful lake Königssee. Both are in the valley below Eagle's Nest.

Location: This monument is high in the Bavarian Alps, roughly 17 miles south of Salzburg and in Germany.

Seasonal Note: This facility is not open in the winter. It is open from mid-May to late October.

How to Get Here: The quickest way to reach the Eagle's Nest from central Salzburg is by car or tour. Driving time is around 40 minutes each way. Buses from central Salzburg require changes and total travel time will likely be more than an hour each way. Tours are the best option as they include reservations to reach the top via the shuttle and elevator system.

> **Important Note for driving in Austria**
>
> You must purchase a **Vignette** and display it on the car windshield. Without this, a steep fine may be incurred. Car rental companies can help with this.

Available Tours: Numerous tours are available. You have choices of half-day tours which only include the Eagle's Nest or full-day tours which will include either a salt mine tour or drive through area countryside. Two of the better companies are Panorama Tours **www.PanoramaTours.com** or Bobs Special Tours **www.BobsTours.com.**

Website: **www.Kehlsteinhaus.de.**

~ ~ ~ ~ ~ ~

Hallstatt, Austria:

Nature of Destination: A stunningly beautiful lakeside town with mountain-top salt mine.

Hallstatt, Austria
Photo Source: Bwag - Wikimedia Commons

Description: Hallstatt's beauty draws many visitors, and it is one of the region's most popular destinations. In addition to the quaint and colorful small town, there is a large salt mine which is easy to reach. Another popular activity is to take a boat across the lake, the Hallstätter See. The one drawback to Hallstatt is the crowds. This is a small town and it brings in visitors from across the globe. A primary attraction is the main street, a short lane lined with colorful alpine lodges and stores.

The mine complex is the Hallstatt Salt World. **www.Saltzwelten.at.** It is the world's oldest salt mine. This mine sits 3,000 feet above the town and there is a skywalk for excellent viewing. Another fun aspect of this trip is a funicular ride up to the top.

A Starting-Point Guide

Hallstatt Salt World Funicular

Location: This small town is southeast from Salzburg. Driving distance is roughly 47 miles.

How to Get Here: The fastest way to reach Hallstatt is by driving or taking one of the many available tours. Travel time by car or tour bus is slightly over one hour. You can take area buses or trains, but in each case, one-way travel time is nearly 2 ½ hours.

Available Tours: This is one of the easiest destinations to find available tours and they are available as half-day or full day. Virtually every area tour company such as Panorama Tours, Viator, or Bobs Special Tours, offers trips to Hallstatt. All tours will include the salt mine. Full day tours often include a visit to nearby Bad Ischl.

Website: www.Hallstatt.net.

~ ~ ~ ~ ~ ~

Königssee, Germany / Lake Königssee:

Nature of Destination: A beautiful alpine lake surrounded by steep mountains with enjoyable boat tours and mountain hikes.

Enjoy a boat trip on Lake Königssee

Description: It is impossible to overstate the beauty of this natural lake and neighboring alpine region. This is one of Germany's deepest lakes and, with the mountain runoff, the waters are delightfully clear. In size, the lake is long and narrow with a length of 4.8 miles (7.7km) providing a lot of area to explore.

Among the available activities here, taking a boat trip the length of the lake should be at the top of the list. These electric boats stop at several points along the way, providing you the opportunity to get out, take a hike, or just relax in a beautiful, natural setting before heading back.

A popular destination on the lake is to get off at the St. Bartholomew pier where there is an attractive 17th century church and a national park with extensive trails.

There are several hiking trails here. A popular one is the Obersee trail which spans for 25 kilometers, a full day's hike. It is a loop so you end up at your starting point. Other trails are available, and information is available at the boat ferry ticket office.

In the attractive village of Königssee, there is a beer garden which provides a good opportunity to kick back and enjoy the scenery while having local beer and treats.

Location: This lake is in Germany, roughly 17 miles south of Salzburg. The starting point for visiting this lake is in the village of Königssee, which sits at the northern end of the lake. The town of Berchtesgaden, which has a large salt mine, is only a 6-minute drive north from here.

How to Get Here: If you have a car available, it is roughly a 40-minute drive to the village of Königssee. There is a parking lot near the lake and ferry dock. Buses are a viable option. To do this, take bus 840 from central Salzburg then, in Berchtesgaden, switch to bus 843. This trip takes around one hour each way.

Available Tours: Few tours only include this lake and village. Most tours will combine a visit with the Eagle's Nest and possibly also the salt mine in Berchtesgaden. Check Viator.com or Panorama Tours (and others) for available tours.

Website: **www.Seenschifffahrt.de** or **www.Berchtesgaden.de** Then scroll down to the link to information on Lake Königssee.

~ ~ ~ ~ ~ ~

Werfen, Austria:

Nature of Destination: Attractive Alpine town with hilltop castle and large ice caves.

The Hohenwerfen Castle overlooks the town of Werfen

Description: Imagine a day where you travel a beautiful route through the mountains to an attractive town where you then explore a magnificent hilltop castle, go in a large ice cave, and even see some of the shooting locations for the *Sound of Music*. This, in a nutshell, outlines a day trip to Warfen.

Werfen has a population of 3,000 and is a pleasant town to stroll and dine in. The big draws here are the fortress and ice caves which are in the hills immediately above the town. In addition to these major attractions on the edge of town, try to take some time to explore the town of Werfen. The town prides itself for its crafts and workshops. The shops and workshops here provide unique handmade items including furniture, shoes, and hats.

Hohenwerfn Castle / Burg Hohenwerfen: Built in the 11th century, this fortress and rock castle sit 2,000 feet above the town. It is defined as a rock castle because it incorporates the rocky outcroppings into its structure and defenses. The fortress and castle belonged to the Habsburg family until it was given over to the state of Salzburg.

Visitors here may join group tours and explore the watch towers, residential quarters and ancient gates, armory, and more. This fortress is operated by the same group that manages the fortress in Salzburg and their tour and ticket offerings have a similar level of complexity. Tickets may be selected which include the lift to the fortress or you may choose to take the steep hike up from the town. Visit. **www.Salzburg-Burgen.at** Then select Burg Hohenwerfn for details and ticket options.

Ice Caves / Eisrienswelt Werfen: This is the world's largest ice cave and is impressive in every regard. The journey begins with a gondola ride up the mountain from the visitor center followed by a dramatic hike to the cave's entrance. Once you are inside the caves, you are taken on a group tour deep into the heart of the mountain to view the numerous ice formations. Full details and ticket options may be found at: **www.Eisriesenwelt.at**.

Sound of Music **Filming Locations:** Some of this popular movie's most noted locations were done here, including the opening hill-top scenes with Julie Andrews. The only way to reach these locations is by tour bus or driving to them. The town's website **www.Werfen.at** provides helpful information on where to find these filming locations and locations for other movies shot here.

Location: The town of Werfen, Austria is 29 miles (46km) due south from Salzburg and is on the Salzach River, the same river which flows through Salzburg.

How to Get Here: The town is a very easy destination to reach by train, bus, and driving. If you are driving, it is an easy 35-minute drive along beautiful roads. Trains travel from Salzburg frequently throughout the day and, depending on the train you select, will take 40 to 55 minutes.

Reaching the castle or ice caves is more complex if you are not driving. The castle sits on a hill above town and may be reached by a steep 30-minute uphill hike, or you can catch a shuttle to the castle at the train station. To reach the Eisriensenwelt ice caves from Werfen, there is a shuttle from the train station which departs frequently during peak season.

Available Tours: The ice caves and castle are popular destinations, and several full-day tours are available from Salzburg. Viator.com and Panorama Tours are good options for this adventure. In addition to group bus or van tours, there are many private tours available from these same providers. These tours provide the significant advantage of taking you to the castle and ice caves which are in the hills above Werfen.

Website: **www.Werfen.at**.

~ ~ ~ ~ ~ ~

Index of Sights in this Guide

Advent Festival 30
Airport Information 24
Apps to Download............ 6
Attractions Guide............ 56
Bad Ischl, Austria 103
Beer Gardens..................... 88
Bob's Special Tours 48
Burg Hohenwerfen 112
Cathedral.......................... 83
Christmas Market............ 30
Christmas Museum......... 59
City Card 42
Climate by Month 28
Discount Passes 42
Dom zu Salzburg............. 83
DomQuartier.................... 60
Eagle's Nest 105
Eisrienweit Caves.......... 112
Events & Festivals 29
Folk Wear Shops 88
Fortress Hohensalzburg . 61
Fortress Museum............. 64
Funicular 65
Getreidegasse Street........ 66
Grayline Tours.................. 48
Hallein Salt Mine............. 96

Hallstatt Salt World 107
Hallstatt, Austria 107
Hellbrunn Palace............. 67
History Museum 85
Hitler's Eagles Nest 105
Hohenwerfen Castle 111
Hop-On Bus 48
Horse Pond 69
Hotel Guide...................... 32
Ice Caves......................... 112
Karajon Square 69
Konigssee, Germany 109
Lake Konigssee 109
Layout of Salzburg.......... 12
Marionette Museum 70
Mirabell Gardens............. 71
Modern Art Museum...... 74
Mozart Birthplace............ 76
Mozart Concerts 51
Mozart Residence 77
Mozart Square 79
Mozart Week.................... 31
Natural History 80
Neue Residenz................. 85
Old Salt Works................. 98
Panorama Museum......... 82
Panorama Tours 49

Day Trips from Salzburg

Points of Interest 55
Salt Mine Tours 93, 99
Salzburg Card 43
Salzburg Cathedral 83
Salzburg Museum 85
Salzburg Overview 8
Salzburg Palace 60
Salzburg Zoo 86
SalzburgerLand Card 43
Schloss Hellbrunn 67
Sciences Museum 80
Shopping Street 66

Sound of Music Tours 52
Tour Providers 47
Tourist Office 4
Tours to Consider 46
Toy Museum 87
Train Station 21
Traveling to Salzburg 20
Trick Fountains 67
Walking Distances 15
Werfen, Austria 111
Zoo Hellbrunn 86

SALZBURG

Starting-Point Guides

www.StartingPointGuides.com

This guidebook on Salzburg, Austria is one of several current and planned *Starting-Point Guides*. Each book in the series is developed with the concept of using one enjoyable city as your basecamp and then exploring from there.

Current guidebooks are for:

- **Bordeaux, France** and the Gironde Region
- **Dijon, France** and the Burgundy Region.
- **Geneva, Switzerland** and the Lake Geneva area.
- **Gothenburg, Sweden** and the central coast of western Sweden.
- **Lille, France** and the Nord-Pas-de-Calais Area
- **Lucerne, Switzerland**, and the Lake Lucerne region.
- **Lyon, France** and the Saône and Rhône confluence area.
- **Nantes, France** and the western Loire Valley
- **Strasbourg, France** and the central Alsace area.
- **Stuttgart, Germany** and the Baden-Wurttemberg area.
- **Toulouse, France**, and the Haute-Garonne region.

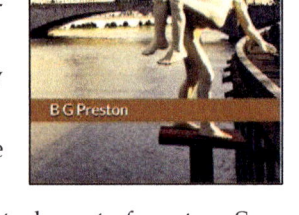

Updates on these and other titles may be found on the author's Facebook page at:

www.Facebook.com/BGPreston.author

Feel free to use this Facebook page to provide feedback and suggestions to the author or email to: cincy3@gmail.com

Printed in Great Britain
by Amazon